BRUGES
TWO THOUSAND YEARS OF HISTORY

NOËL GEIRNAERT - LUDO VANDAMME

English translation by Ted Alkins

Bruges residents and culturally-minded visitors to the city have long expressed a desire for a concise but solid guide to its fascinating history. Stichting Kunstboek has responded to their wishes by producing this book.

Noël Geirnaert, archivist at the Bruges Municipal Archive, and Ludo Vandamme, researcher at the Department of Historical Collections at the Bruges City Library, are the authors of this engaging account of our city's history from the beginning of the first millennium to the present day.
They recount the historical background of our numerous monuments while also examining more recent developments, though always from a historian's perspective. Their fascinating text is supported by a series of fine illustrations.

The book highlights the leading role that Bruges has often played on the Flemish and European stage. This is both a source of justifiable pride and a spur to restore our city to the status it once enjoyed.
The vicissitudes of Bruges' past remind us that immense effort and energy have always been needed to maintain our cultural individuality and economic vigour. This is as true today as it has ever been.

I am convinced that this new Bruges book fills an important niche. It is solidly grounded without becoming bogged down in the myriad details required by a reference book or specialist study. And it is illustrative without being just another attractive photo album.

At the end of the day, it is up to the readers to judge, but I am sure lovers of Bruges will be well satisfied by this fine new publication.

Patrick MOENAERT
Burgomaster of Bruges

The Dijver

FROM EARLY SETTLEMENT
TO INTERNATIONAL TRADING CENTRE.
TWELVE CENTURIES OF HISTORY

Every year, thousands of visitors and residents stroll along the river Dijver, as it flows between the Gruuthuse and Johannes Nepomucenus bridges. This oldest part of the city has probably been inhabited since the beginning of the first millennium A.D. The Dijver once bounded the northern edge of an island covered with oak trees. Celtic etymology suggests that the name of the river meant holy water, and oak forests, too, were believed to be the home of supernatural beings. We know from early mediaeval handbooks of penance that people used to make offerings to oak trees and springs during ceremonial meals here. Ancient practices of this kind were Celtic in origin. This tells us that Bruges must have been a place of worship since pre-Germanic times.
Gallo-Roman Bruges has increasingly given up its secrets in the past twenty years, as research has gained momentum. We now know that people have lived on the site of the modern city since the first century A.D. The Gallo-Roman settlement was a commercial centre until at least 270, maintaining relations with Britain and the rest of Gaul. A Gallo-Roman presence in Bruges has been detected in the northern part of the city, around what is now Fort Lapin and Lange Rei, but traces have also been found in the middle of the modern city centre at the Burg, in Zilverstraat, and near several of the city gates. No remains have yet been found of any Gallo-Roman buildings, but we know that there was a large farm complex on Zandstraat in the Sint-Andries district, barely three kilometres to the north-west of the city centre. And excavations carried out in 1996 established that this settlement already existed in the Celtic period, even before the Roman presence in our region.

The Flemish coast fell victim to Germanic raids in around 270, and the Gallo-Roman settlement is unlikely to have escaped their effects. It might, indeed, have taken on a military character by the late third and fourth century, with Roman fortifications of the kind found in Aardenburg and Oudenburg. No traces of a *castellum* have been found but if one did exist, it will have been located in the earliest nucleus of the town. According to one unsubstantiated but plausible hypothesis, the late-Roman fortification was located in the middle of the square island between the (now covered) Kraanrei, Spiegelrei, Sint-Annarei and Groene Rei. Another theory places it at the Oude Burg, which would then have occupied a greater area than the street that currently bears that name.

There is good reason to suppose that Gallo-Roman Bruges survived the Dark Ages. When Saint Eloy came to the region to preach Christianity in the mid-seventh century, one of his focuses, according to the account of his life written in the first decades of the eighth century, was the *municipium Flandrense*, probably a reference to Bruges. If so, the town was already fortified, definitely Roman in origin and of more than merely local importance. It was the capital of the *Pagus Flandrensis*, the coastal region stretching from the mouth of the river IJzer to Bruges itself. This capital was the residence of the Merovingian count who represented royal authority. Three large royal estates were located around the fortress Snellegem, Weinebrugge (Sint-Michiels) and Sijsele. If Bruges was, indeed, the *municipium Flandrense*, it functioned as the military and administrative centre of the region. It also appears to have traded fairly intensively with Scandinavia.

Bruges actually owes its name to these commercial ties with the north. The original name of the settlement derived from the word *Rugja*, the early name of the Reie, the river which still runs through the heart of the city. The name of the town underwent a remarkable linguistic development in the eighth and first half of the ninth century under the influence of Old Norse. The Scandinavian word *bryggja*, meaning landing place or jetty merged with the original *Rugja*, to form the earliest version of the city's modern name. *Bruggia* first appears on a number of coins struck in Bruges during the regime of Charles the Bald (840-878) which bear dates between 864 and 875. Several surviving examples

Carolingian coins struck in Bruges between 864 and 875
(Bruges, Gruuthuse Museum)

are to be found in the municipal collection and are displayed at
the Gruuthuse Museum.

The outlines of Bruges history thus begin to emerge from the
ninth century onwards. It was in this period that the town
became part of the coastal defences developed by the
Carolingians to protect their territories against the Vikings.
The earliest mediaeval fortress was already in existence in
851, as monks from Saint Bavo's Abbey in Ghent are recorded
as having deposited their valuables there for safe-keeping.
The fortress was probably the residence of Baldwin Iron Arm,
the first count of Flanders whom we know by name. Ten years
later, Baldwin made a dramatic entrance into the annals of
history when he eloped with Judith, daughter of King Charles
the Bald. Baldwin I seemingly managed to stave off the Vikings,
as there is no evidence that Bruges was plundered in the
ninth century. It is also possible that the town still enjoyed
its commercial relations with Scandinavia, from where
the Norsemen launched their attacks.

The first modest fortress at Bruges (covering around one hectare)
stood where the old Roman road from Oudenburg to Aardenburg
crossed the Reie. It is clear that it was located on the site of what
is now the Burg, but its exact position has not been determined.

In addition to valuables from Ghent in 851, relics of Saint Donatian were also brought to Bruges from Torhout between 863 and 871. A number of clerics from Torhout probably came too, seeking protection against the Vikings. The fortress was located on a much larger, square island, which some archaeologists believe to have been the site of the old Roman fortifications. This extended for a total of around sixteen hectares, with the former Saint Walburga's Church at its centre, on the corner of what is now Riddersstraat and Sint-Walburgastraat. The church was demolished in 1781 and was originally the first chapel of the count. It certainly existed by the tenth century. Perhaps Baldwin I housed the relics of Saint Donatian and the Torhout clerics there.

Visitors to the Burg can see the remains of another demolished church, Saint Donatian's, which was destroyed during the period of French annexation (1799-1802). Count Baldwin II (879-918) consolidated and extended comital power, while his son Arnulf I (918-965) enjoyed a long reign during which he laid the foundations for the development of the County of Flanders. Arnulf also gave shape to the Burg in Bruges by having Saint Donatian's Church built there, having first founded a chapter of canons shortly before 944. Arnulf's new castle-church was a late-Carolingian edifice with sixteen sides, modelled on the Palace Chapel in Aachen. He also gave the Burg its final square shape, covering over one and a half hectares, with its ecclesiastical half to the north, dominated by Saint Donatian's, and the count's half to the south. The latter included the original residence of the count to the west.

The large square island, of which the Burg only occupied a small part, was formed by the present Spiegelrei, Sint-Annarei, Groene Rei and Kraanrei. It was probably one of the earliest parts of the modern city to have been inhabited. Cordouaniersstraat and Wapenmakersstraat are located near the Burg, suggesting that the cordwainers and armourers who once lived and worked here were chiefly employed by the count and his soldiers.

Saint Walburga's Church, which continued to serve as the count's chapel until the thirteenth century, stood in the middle of the island. The early-mediaeval harbour, reached via Lange Rei, and the earliest trading settlement were also located here, suggesting that Saint Walburga's functioned as the community's church from a very early date. It might have been from this first settlement that contacts were maintained with the Scandinavian world until the tenth century.

The Oude Burg was a second residential nucleus alongside the Burg. The district originally lay between Streenstraat and the street now known as Oude Burg, and was the centre of domestic trade. The growth of the city between the Markt and the Zand occurred from this part of the city until around 1100.

Bruges' two oldest parish churches are thus located between the Oude Burg and the Zand. Prior to their foundation, the

Remains of Saint Donatian's Church (c. 950) now incorporated in the Burg Hotel (Holiday Inn Crowne Plaza)

ecclesiastical structure had taken no account of the nucleus of the town's expansion nor of the growing population of Bruges. The oldest churches in the region were located several kilometres outside the town in the old Merovingian royal estates of Sijsele and Snellegem, and at Sint-Michiels in Weinebrugge, founded in around 800. Sint-Michiels (Saint Michael's) parish was created as an offshoot of Snellegem. In the same period, the parish of Sint-Kruis (Sacred Cross) was created out of Sijsele, stretching as far as Sint-Annarei and Potterierei until 1668. Sacred Cross might have been founded to minister to the population of the growing town. The Parish of Our Lady will then have split off from Sijsele when it became apparent that the town was developing in a different direction (to the south-west of Saint Walburga's district).

The first reference to Our Lady's as a parish church is to be found in a text dating from 1089. However, the earliest church building probably dates from the second half of the ninth century. It was originally a daughter church of Saint Martin's in Sijsele, and so belonged to Saint Martin's Chapter in Utrecht, even though Sijsele and Bruges belonged to the bishopric of Tournai throughout the Middle Ages. Holy Saviour's is undoubtedly the oldest parish church in Bruges. The earliest surviving reference to it is in a bull issued by Pope John XV in 988. Holy Saviour's was created from the parish of Sint-Michiels in Weinebrugge, probably in the ninth century. According to legend, it was founded by Saint Eloy himself in the seventh century, but there is no truth in this, any more than in the story that the parish of Our Lady was created by Saint Boniface. The third Bruges parish church was Saint Donatian's, which was granted this status in 1089. The parish of Saint Donatian was limited to the area of the Burg. Bruges thus had two genuine urban parish churches by the end of the eleventh century. They were actually located on the edge of the town, as they were originally founded from two rural parishes and no doubt functioned initially as secondary institutions. Several new parishes grew out of the original two in the thirteenth century.

The foundation of two new parishes in around 1000 A.D. was a natural consequence of the rapid economic and demographic growth experienced by the town. Bruges had already been the residence of the count, Baldwin I and his successors, for over a century and had become a port and a commercial centre of European standing by the beginning of the eleventh century. This view is supported by an anonymous English text written in 1040-42, which describes Bruges as a town of many merchants offering a vast range of goods for sale. It also states that ships sailed from England and moored in Bruges. Trade with England might already have been established for over a century by this time.

Bruges was directly accessible from the sea between the Roman era and the eleventh century. Ships could probably even reach the centre of the town via Lange Rei. In the second half of the eleventh century, however, the natural link with the sea silted up as a result of land reclamation carried out to the north of the town. This had the effect of shifting the focus of commercial activity and urban development from maritime trade to commerce by land. Overland trade alone, however, would not have enabled Bruges to maintain its position as an international commercial centre. Fortunately, a major flood along the coast of Flanders and Zealand in 1134 created a deep, new channel as far as what is now Damme. A canal was duly excavated to link Bruges to this new channel, known as the Zwin. Goods destined for Bruges had, however, to be transferred to smaller vessels at Damme. Left alone, the Zwin would gradually have silted up again, and so the channel via Damme had to be dredged from the late thirteenth century onwards. Even so, the creation of the Zwin established Bruges' maritime role until the fifteenth century, although the port was destined to expand via a series of out-ports like Damme, followed later by Hoeke, Monnikerede and Sluis. In the thirteenth century, Bruges became the economic capital of north-western Europe. The following chapter of this book is devoted to the city's commercial heyday.

Several other developments occurred before 1200, the traces of which are still visible in Bruges today. What's more, a remarkable source survives from the early twelfth century, offering a unique insight into the town in that period. In the early hours of Wednesday 2 March 1127, Count Charles the Good was brutally murdered as he sat praying in Saint Donatian's Church. The murder of the count caused universal uproar. Galbert of Bruges, clerk and canon at Saint Donatian's, kept a diary of the events. His fascinating eye-witness account includes a wealth of information concerning Bruges at that time. According to Galbert, news of the murder reached London and Laon within two days – a fact he later learned from local merchants who had been in London and students from the cathedral school in Laon, one of western Europe's leading centres of higher education. Galbert himself is likely to have studied at Laon, where many Bruges clerics were shaped intellectually. The rapid spread of the news of Charles murder shows how well integrated Bruges was in the western European commercial and cultural network. Galbert's account of the events in 1127 and 1128 tells us that Flanders in general and Bruges in particular were plunged into a deep crisis. The count's assassins belonged to the powerful Erembald clan, headed by Bertulf, dean of the chapter of Saint Donatian. The clan had long dominated the Flemish administration, exercising a great deal of influence from its headquarters on the Burg. But its power-base was very small, and the family were not freemen, which meant Charles the Good would inevitably have acted sooner or later to curtail their ambition. To prevent this from happening, the Erembalds had the count murdered. Rather than profiting from their crime, however, they fell victim to the ruthless reprisals that ensued. The battle for the succession initially looked set to be won by William Clito, the candidate of the French king. After twelve months had passed, though, it became plain that Thierry of Alsace, supported by Ghent and Bruges, would become the new count.
These events clearly showed that Flanders had become an independent territory by 1127 and 1128, and that it had assumed particular importance on the international stage.

It is apparent, too, that economic power within the territory lay with the wealthy merchants of towns like Bruges and Ghent. The period also witnessed the emergence of a number of political issues that were to dominate the history of Bruges and Flanders for centuries to come – the county's autonomy and its relationship with France, the role of the towns in Flemish politics and the balance of power within them.

It was in that turbulent year of 1127 that the citizens of Bruges wrested their first charter from William Clito, the most likely contender for the countship. Before the citizens of Bruges would recognise him, they insisted he meet a number of conditions. So it was that the town was granted formal autonomy. It was probably at this point that Bruges gained its first council, with explicit powers and a specific jurisdiction. The text of the first charter has been lost, but Galbert is emphatic that such a document existed. Bruges was granted a revised charter some fifty years later, between 1165 and 1177, this time by Count Philip of Alsace. The text of the second charter has survived and begins by briefly summarising the town's territory.

The latter had already been established in 1127. In the aftermath of the murder of Charles the Good, the citizens threw up a defensive wall round the city which was to mark its boundaries for some two centuries. The position of those early fortifications can still be identified. They followed the inner canals, which already existed for the most part in 1127, and which still partially feature in the modern cityscape – Sint-Annarei to the east, followed by Groene Rei and the Dijver, Kapucijnenrei, Smedenrei, Speelmansrei and Augustijnenrei. The fortifications incorporated six city gates, none of which have survived, although a tower belonging to the original defences can still be seen in the garden wall of a house in Pieter Pourbusstraat, visible from Pottenmakersstraat. Few residents or visitors are aware of its origins. The area known as the Zand was still located beyond the city walls at that time, but Galbert tells us that the citizens used to congregate there for important meetings and executions. The Markt, or marketplace, was located in the centre of the town and was also used for assemblies and executions. Saint Christopher's Church stood at the centre of the marketplace where the modern-day Markt borders the Eiermarkt. It was demolished in the eighteenth century. Saint Peter's Chapel, just off the Burg, has survived. The building probably dates from the eleventh century. The town was intersected by several important roads. The two principal highways, one to Ghent and one to Ypres and Lille, met at what is now Simon Stevinplein. Some historians believe that this was the site of the original marketplace. Whatever the case, the majority of Bruges' population in around 1100 lived in this district. The road to Aardenburg and Antwerp lay to the east, past the Burg, continuing on from the Ypres road.

Galbert chiefly lived and worked on the Burg, and it was there, too, that most of the key events in his story took place. His description of the square tallies with what we know already. The southern half of the Burg was fundamentally altered in the course of the twelfth century. The count's residence, originally located to the west, was shifted to the east, where the Liberty of Bruges building now stands. Count Thierry of Alsace built Saint Basil's Church between 1134 and 1157. The building is better known as the Chapel of the Holy Blood, as it has housed the relic of that name since the first half of the thirteenth century. Although local legend has it that Thierry brought the Holy Blood from Jerusalem to Bruges, it probably came from Constantinople and was brought back by Count Baldwin IX, who served as Emperor of the eastern city between May 1204 and April 1205. Saint Basil's has been a double church since its construction. Only the lower part has retained its impressive Romanesque character. The upper church had fallen into acute disrepair by 1810, prompting its fundamental restoration in the first half of the nineteenth century.

A key welfare institution created in twelfth-century Bruges has survived to the present day. Saint John's Hospital once stood on the edge of the town, near the Mariapoort, one of the original city gates. It is located opposite Our Lady's Church, where the

Remains of the first city walls, viewed from Pottenmakersstraat

important road to Kortrijk and Ghent left the city. The earliest documentary reference to the hospital dates from 1188, but it is plain that Saint John's had already been in existence for several years. It treated the sick and injured, and cared for needy passers-by, vagrants, pilgrims, homeless people and the mentally ill. The foundation of such an institution, which was administered by the city council, is indicative of the vigorous growth of Bruges' population in the twelfth century.

This chapter began with a reference to the Dijver and the oak-covered island it bordered. The area lay just outside the town limits from 1127 onwards, retaining its religious character even after the region's conversion to Christianity. A hermit called Everelmus settled there in around 1050, living a life of piety and retreat until his death in 1060, during which time he earned a reputation for holiness. So it was that the earliest pre-Christian place of worship was able to retain its sacred character.
The hermitage and Everelmus tomb later became a place of pilgrimage. A community of devout men and women grew up there in the twelfth century. The male members remained and duly founded a community of canons regular (Eekhout Abbey) which survived until the end of the eighteenth century.
The women moved to Assebroek, where they founded Saint Trudo's Abbey, which stands to this day in the grounds of Male castle.

*Romanesque tympanum with the Baptism of Christ,
12th century, Saint Basil's Church (Chapel of the Holy Blood)*

THE BURG

The Burg in Bruges: from count's fortress to modern city centre.
So ran the title of an academic report published in 1991, which
provided a detailed account of recent archaeological research
at the Burg. The title summed up the historical development of
this fine public space. Tourist guides in Bruges like to begin
their tours at the pedestrianised square, which is surrounded by
representatives of virtually all European architectural styles, from
pre-Romanesque to post-modern. Nowadays, the buildings that
fringe the Burg are painstakingly cared for by historians, archaeologists, art-historians and conservationists, but that was not always
the case. Barely ten years ago, archaeologists had to fight hard
to save the monumental remains of an old fortress wall and
Saint Donatian's Church during the construction of the new hotel
complex. The Romanesque tower on the north-west corner of
Saint Donatian's was demolished as recently as 1963.
The greatest damage, however, was inflicted at the end of
the eighteenth century by French revolutionary troops.
Saint Donatian's, the seat of the bishop of Bruges since 1559,
was entirely demolished and the materials sold off. Heaps of
rubble remained on the site for years, serving as a vantage
point from which the city's children were able to glimpse Emperor
Napoleon and Empress Marie-Louise during their visit in May
1810. Some years previously, French revolutionaries and their
supporters in Bruges had smashed the statues on the facade

of the Town Hall and the Chapel of the Holy Blood had been allowed to fall into disrepair.

Their attitude was historically understandable. The Burg had come to epitomise the Ancien Régime, every conceivable symbol of which had accumulated around it in the course of a millennium. Before the French period, the square had marked the beginning and end of Bruges' Holy Blood Processions and similar events to honour the city's patron saints. It was here that judgement was passed and torture and executions staged. More or less all the city's institutions had their headquarters on the Burg. The Town Hall was here, with the civil and criminal courts, the seat of the Liberty of Bruges, the deanery of Saint Donatian's and the collegial chamber of the extensive lordship of Sijsele. Symbols, emblems, statues and coats of arms accreted around the buildings, lending a religious air to the exercise of power and authority that was further heightened by the presence of Saint Donatian's Church and its clergy – canons, chaplains and, from 1562, a bishop. The Burg perfectly symbolised the linkage between Church and State at the end of the eighteenth century. The French occupation (1795-1814) resulted in its dismantling, both literal and figurative, followed by the refashioning of the square in the nineteenth century. The Burg remained an ecclesiastical, judicial and administrative centre until the late twentieth century, thanks to the presence of the Chapel of the Holy Blood and of the law courts in the former palace of the Liberty of Bruges (until 1984). Nevertheless, the religious veneer it had once added to the exercise of power and authority had disappeared forever.

WATER IN THE BRUGES CITYSCAPE

Bruges owes its name and foundation as a trading settlement to the Reie, the river that flows through the city from the Minnewater to Dampoort, and to its role as a mooring for ships seeking a haven from the sea. Bruges *reien*, the name given to its canals, are now one of the city's principal attractions. Their precise origins however, the extent to which they are natural or man-made, present historians and archaeologists with a knotty problem. It is entirely possible that the Gallo-Roman people who lived here in the first two centuries A.D. had already begun to alter the pattern of the local waterways.

The river enters the city at the Minnewater, mistakenly translated by nineteenth-century romantics as the 'Lac d'Amour'. Historians suggested in the past that the name really means 'common water', but this, too, is probably incorrect. A more recent linguistic explanation is that minnewater originally meant 'water where a sprite lives'. If this is true, the Minnewater does not date from the twelfth or thirteenth century, but is much older and was not created artificially. Lange Rei and Spiegelrei – the final stretch of the river within the current city centre – probably follow the natural watercourse, too. The same goes for the Dijver, the name of which is pre-Germanic in origin. It is also believed that the canals at the Beguinage, Saint John's

Hospital and Rozenhoedkaai follow the original course of
the river Reie. It is less clear to what extent the other canals
in Bruges are natural in origin. Human intervention is more
likely in this case.
The earliest fortifications (from Speelmansrei, via Augustijnenrei,
Gouden Handrei and Verwersdijk to Groene Rei) are probably
a combination of human intervention and natural watercourses.
The second set of defences, running for almost seven kilometres
and consisting of double canals, was created at the end of the
thirteenth century and is entirely artificial. Part of these defences
was incorporated in the eighteenth century in the canal linking
Ghent with Ostend. The final visible addition to Bruges waterways is the canal known as the Coupure, which dates from
1751-53. It was excavated to reduce the length of the journey
across town between Dampoort and the Ghent canal. A new
town dock, the Handelskom, had been excavated at Dampoort,
just outside the city's defences, a century earlier. The same spot
marked the termination at the time of the canal linking Bruges
with Ostend.
We have only referred in this brief round-up to the waterways
that are still visible in Bruges today. Many canals and
embankments have been covered or filled in over the years.
The most important were Pandreitje, filled in in 1768, Kraanrei,
which ran as far as the Markt and was covered over in three
stages, 1787-88, 1793-95 and 1856, and Komvest, filled in
in 1897.

BRUGES: ECONOMIC CAPITAL
OF NORTH-WESTERN EUROPE, 1200-1400

The mediaeval county of Flanders was one of the most urbanised regions in Europe. Only northern and central Italy were more developed in this respect. The process peaked in Flanders in the thirteenth century and does not appear to have advanced any further in the remainder of the Middle Ages. By the mid-fourteenth century, the population of Bruges stood between 40,000 and 45,000, twice the level of the modern inner city. It is likely, furthermore, that the town had just as many, if not more, inhabitants a hundred years earlier. The thirteenth century was a period of economic growth in Bruges and Flanders. In 1316, however, the region was struck by a major famine and in 1349 by an outbreak of plague. Disasters of this kind were uncommon in the thirteenth century.

Like other Flemish towns, Bruges was a large-scale textile producer, even before 1200, using both local and English wool. Woollen textiles were then exported all over Europe. References to this business have been found in Spanish and Italian sources from the thirteenth century. Wool imports, cloth production and cloth exports were controlled in Bruges by a rich entrepreneur class, on whom craftsmen were dependent at every stage of the production process. The same merchants and entrepreneurs also dominated the city administration. They were grouped together in the London Hansa, the organisation of Bruges merchants trading with England. In the second half of the thirteenth century, craftsmen and other members of the middle class began to join the Hansa, too, simultaneously giving them a say in the governing of the city. It was around this period that the monopoly of the merchant-entrepreneurs was broken and a new type of small businessman arose. Some craftsmen became entrepreneurs in their own right, taking on a limited number of workers with different specialist skills. Bruges

Belfry and market-halls on the Markt. 13th-century complex crowned
by an octagonal upper section from the 15th century (see pp. 31-32)

differed from the other Flemish towns, certainly from around 1250, in the size of its middle class. The difference was heightened by the fact that towns like Ghent, Ypres and Douai were purely industrial, or rather textile centres, whereas Bruges was an international trading hub that had developed a more diverse range of activities. An important annual market had been held there from around 1200, and in the final quarter of the thirteenth century, the city became the pre-eminent centre of international trade in north-western Europe. It was in this period that predominantly overland transport gave way to transport by sea.

Despite this prosperity, thirteenth-century Bruges, like other towns in Flanders, also had a great many poor people, who lived in immense hardship. Social tension sometimes spilled over into unrest, as occurred during the Moerlemaye of October 1280. In the run-up to the troubles, the Belfry was seriously damaged by fire, destroying the town's archive and with it the documents setting out its privileges. The count of Flanders showed little inclination to renew the city's charter, and decided instead to take the opportunity to consolidate his authority over Bruges and the other Flemish towns. Members of the urban elite were thus pitted against the count. Their dissatisfaction had already been aroused by the departure of foreign merchants in the summer of 1280 to Aardenburg, where they were granted more generous privileges by Count Guy of Dampierre. Around 1 October 1280, a group of prominent burghers mounted a coup within the city council, supported by the ordinary populace. Members of the previous regime fled or were imprisoned, and their houses were plundered and burned. A list of grievances was presented to Robert of Bethune, the count's son, on behalf of the people. Within the space of a year, however, the rebellion had been crushed and a heavy price exacted from the town. The new charter issued on 25 May 1281 consolidated the power of the count and curtailed that of the town council. A subsequent revolt in the summer of 1281 was crushed even more ruthlessly. A new era in the social history of Bruges and Flanders was not destined to begin until 1302.

Steady economic growth caused Bruges to burst its seams in the thirteenth century. The original fortifications, erected in 1127, were no longer able to function as the city's boundaries. Available land outside the walls was rapidly divided into building plots. The new districts consisted primarily of small, one-room dwellings for the city's labourers, while spacious townhouses were built inside the old walls. Bruges oldest surviving stone frontages date from around 1300 (Grauwwerkersstraat 2-4 and Jan van Eyckplein 6, for instance). The city authorities banned thatched roofs in certain districts shortly before 1232 to reduce the danger of fire. Two centuries later, in 1417, following several major conflagrations on the edge of the city, a scheme was set up whereby subsidies were offered to householders who replaced their thatched roofs with tiles. Wooden houses remained common in the mediaeval town, and their building and renovation was not prohibited until the seventeenth century. Only two such buildings now survive, Kortewinkel 2 and Genthof 7.

The town proper, that is, the area governed by the city aldermen, was largely limited until the third quarter of the thirteenth century to the territory lying within the old fortifications, although the Braamberg district, to the south of Groene Rei, was added to the town some time before 1246. In the period after 1275, the city boundaries were not only adjusted to take account of the altered circumstances, its territory was significantly expanded with a view to further population growth. Some of the count's officials placed ten boundary posts around the city, marking out its area in an entirely arbitrary manner. They deliberately took no account of existing roads, waterways or other landmarks. New fortifications were built in 1297, delineating an area that was to remain unchanged until 1795. They still mark the boundaries of the inner city and are clearly visible in the modern cityscape. This second set of defences enclosed an area measuring 431 hectares and with a circumference of 6,800 metres. The final city walls and stone gates were not added until a hundred years later. Four of the nine gates survive to this day – Ezelpoort, built in 1369-70, Gentpoort, built in 1361-63 and rebuilt in 1401-06, Kruispoort, built in 1366-68 and partially rebuilt in 1401-06 and Smedenpoort, built in 1367-68 and partially rebuilt in 1615. All that remains of the defensive towers is the Poertoren which stands by the Minnewater. It was built in 1398, and owes its name to the fact that it was used to produce and store gunpowder from the fifteenth century onwards. It was also in the thirteenth century that Bruges was given its first, rudimentary water supply. Lead pipes carried drinking water from the city reservoir at Saint Bavo's (now the Sint-Andries district) to a number of public wells. The reservoir ceased to be used in around 1385, when it was replaced by a pumping station in the moat at Smedenpoort. The mediaeval Waterhuis (waterhouse) on Hendrik Consciencelaan survives to this day.

The growth of the city in the thirteenth century is apparent from the development of the ecclesiastical structure in that period. Mendicant Orders began to found monasteries in the major urban centres. Bruges had no fewer than six male and two female foundations of this kind. Oddly, Bruges (approximately 45,000 inhabitants in the fourteenth century) had a larger number of monasteries and convents and more friars and nuns than Ghent (64,000 inhabitants). Wealthy industrial Ghent evidently provided fewer opportunities for mendicants than rich, commercial Bruges. Franciscans, Dominicans, Augustinians, Carmelites, Brothers of the Sack and Magpie Brothers all had monasteries in Bruges. Franciscan and Dominican nuns, too, were based in or immediately outside the city. All that remains of these institutions, however, are a few traces of the mediaeval Dominican monastery incorporated in a modern apartment building near Predikheren Bridge. The monasteries and convents of the mendicant Orders left little mark on the cityscape, but their influence cannot be overstated. The cosmopolitan nature of the mendicants meant that they had a great deal of contact with foreign merchants. As the fourteenth century progressed, therefore, many groups of foreign traders set up chapels in the mendicants' churches. English merchants began to use the Carmelites' refectory as their meeting place in 1334. Traders belonging to the German Hansa kept a little chest containing their standard weights in the Franciscans' dormitory from 1347, one of the keys to which was kept at the Carmelite monastery. The first manuscripts containing miniatures inspired by Franciscan and Dominican doctrine appear in Bruges in around 1250. In other words, the mendicants also contributed to the first works of art produced in Bruges to boast more than regional importance.

The mendicant Orders responded more quickly to the new pastoral needs of the growing urban population than the established secular clergy. Even so, Bruges parish structure was adjusted in the second quarter of the thirteenth century. Remarkably, the town's thirteenth-century parish churches have virtually all survived. Only the earliest, Saint Walburga's, which began as the count's chapel and became a parish church in 1239, has disappeared. The parish of Saint James (Sint-Jacobs) was founded in 1240 out of the existing parish of Holy Saviour. Old Saint James's Chapel, near the Ezelpoort (also known as Sint-Jacobspoort) in the city's original fortifications, became the new parish church. It was rapidly transformed into an early-Gothic cross-shaped church, before being altered again two centuries later to create the building we know today with its three aisles. The block tower of Saint James's Church is early-Gothic and dates from the thirteenth and fourteenth century. The parish of Saint Giles was founded in 1241, or shortly before, from Our Lady's. Its parish church was an early-Gothic building that was fundamentally altered in the late Middle Ages. Nowadays, it is a three-aisled hall church with few remnants of the original cross-shaped building. The solid tower, like that of Saint James, lends it a rather squat silhouette of the type seen in early-Gothic churches in the polders.

Existing churches were also altered to accommodate the city's growing population, with the exception of Saint Donatian's, which was rebuilt after a major fire in 1184. A few traces in the lowest part of the present tower are all that now remains of the Romanesque Holy Saviour's. Construction of the new church began in the final quarter of the thirteenth century, although the work continued until the first half of the sixteenth century. Our Lady's, which had been remodelled in the Romanesque style in the twelfth century, was rebuilt again as a Gothic church, beginning in the thirteenth century. The new building, with its 120 metre-high tower, was finished in around 1350. The Holy Blood relic was stored in Saint Basil's Church from the first half of the thirteenth century, having been presented to the city by the count some time before 1250. The annual Holy Blood Procession first appears in the city's annals in the thirteenth century.

The Begijnhof (beguinage) draws thousands of visitors a year to enjoy its atmosphere of peace and contemplation in the midst of the city's bustle. It, too, dates from the thirteenth century. A community of pious women were living at the Wijngaard beguinage in 1244, when the bishop of Tournai granted it independent parish status. Its own church was opened in 1245. Countess Margaret of

De Wijngaard beguinage, founded in the 13th century.
The present buildings are about four centuries more recent.

Constantinople had the viscount's chapel moved from the Burg to the beguinage. The institution was removed from the city's authority in 1299, when King Philip IV of France placed it under the direct control of the sovereign, hence its title Prinselijk Begijnhof (Prince's Beguinage). The present buildings are not mediaeval, but date largely from the seventeenth century.

Few surviving civic buildings in Bruges were built in the thirteenth century, although Saint John's Hospital, which dates from the twelfth century, was given the first of its three wards in the early 1200s. Together with the western facade of Our Lady's, it continues to dominate Mariastraat at the Maria Bridge. The hospital's Romanesque tower was built in the same period. The two other wards were added at the end of the thirteenth century (the north ward) and in 1309-10 (the south ward). The hospital brothers were given new accommodation near the north ward. Their monastery also dates from the beginning of the fourteenth century. The present convent is over two hundred years more recent. Saint John's Hospital, with its estate of over four hectares, was very much a civic institution, but that did not prevent the bishop of Tournai from attempting to establish his authority over it in 1236. The city's aldermen managed, however, to retain full control until the third quarter of the fifteenth century. They ruled in 1236 that the estates of deceased patients and members of staff should be inherited by the hospital. The first reference to the governors who ran Saint John's on behalf of the city occurs in a document dating from 1270.

The belfry and market hall on the Markt are the second large complex of buildings dating from the thirteenth century. The first wooden market hall was constructed here no later than the early 1200s. The stone hall probably dates from around 1240. The earliest belfry is unlikely to have been built much later. The market hall was, of course, used for commercial purposes, while the city aldermen used to meet in the chamber in the belfry. The municipal council, treasury and archive containing Bruges privileges were all centred here, as were the city's bells. The belfry thus served as a clear symbol of municipal autonomy. The fire of 1280 probably did a great deal of damage internally, but the building was far from completely destroyed. The aldermen did, however, move to the Burg, where they occupied the Ghiselhuus on the site of the later Town Hall. The count, meanwhile, resided less and less frequently at the Burg and the castle at Male developed into the principal comital residence near Bruges.

The final years of the thirteenth and the first years of the fourteenth century were crucial to the history of Bruges and Flanders. The French king, Philip IV, annexed the county in 1297. The majority of wealthy urbanites, including the burghers of Bruges, sided with the French against Count Guy of Dampierre. Bruges pledged allegiance to Philip on 18 September 1297. The entire county was occupied by the French in 1300, during which period the second set of city defences was installed. Philip IV and his wife, Joan of Navarra, visited Bruges in late May and early June 1301. The population of the city received them very coolly, not least because the Francophile city council had strictly forbidden the people to ask the royal couple for special tax privileges. Resistance broke out almost immediately the visitors had departed. Pieter de Coninc, a sixty-year-old weaver, was the ring-leader, and Jan Breydel, a well-to-do butcher, was another key figure in the resistance movement. Two of the count's younger sons, John and Guy of Namur, and his grandson, William of Gulik, added their military might. Pieter de Coninc seized power in Bruges in 1302, and Guy of Namur and William of Gulik entered the town in March. Within two months, however, the French and their supporters were back in control. The resistance recaptured the town in the early morning of 18 May. This event, in the course of which 1,500 Frenchmen and their supporters were killed, became known as the 'Bruges Matins'. The larger part of the county was subsequently reconquered from Bruges.

The conflict culminated in victory over the French at the Battle of the Golden Spurs near Kortrijk on 11 July 1302, the seven-hundredth anniversary of which will be celebrated in a few years time. Bruges provided no fewer than 2,380 troops – the largest single

Statue of Jan Breydel and Pieter de Coninc, unveiled in 1887 (Markt)

contingent. Some 2,060 members of the militia were craftsmen, with 320 cavalrymen from the city's burgher class. The involvement of the latter indicates that the struggle against the French and their supporters in Bruges was not simply a matter for the craftsmen. The latter were, however, granted greater autonomy in which to organise their affairs after the victory. The new city charter which followed also gave the guilds more of a say in the government of Bruges.

The war with France dragged on until 1305, when it was concluded by the Treaty of Athis-sur-Orge, which was very unfavourable to Flanders. Bruges was obliged to pay a heavy fine and to dismantle its defences. The city responded defiantly, seeking to spin out its compliance for as long as possible. Bruges suffered further setbacks, however. Famine struck in 1316, following the failure of the previous year's harvest, costing the lives of between five and ten percent of the population. Economic adversity, accompanied by political and social unrest, were to mark the entire fourteenth century. Low-points occurred in 1328, when Bruges was made to pay for its support of the Flemish peasants' revolt, the period 1349-50 following a Europe-wide plague epidemic, and in the year 1382, when the Flemish cities were defeated at the battle of Westrozebeke by Count Louis of Male and his French allies. The subsequent repression culminated in 224 executions in Bruges.

None of this altered the fact that fourteenth-century Bruges was the most prosperous city in the county of Flanders. With a population of around 40,000, it was a major local market in its own right. Craftsmen in the textile sector boasted immense technical skills and their products grew increasingly refined. Large volumes of textiles were also produced in the town's hinterland of Flanders, Brabant and Artois, exports from which occurred entirely through Bruges. All manner of artistic production had developed in the city, providing foreign merchants with a varied range of products. A fifth of Bruges population in 1340 was employed as tailors, skilled craftsmen or utensil makers. A quarter was active in the wholesale trade, the money market or as broker-hoteliers. Bruges developed into a major international market in the fourteenth century with a highly varied local supply and an extremely advanced financial system.

The latter is worthy of particular attention. The availability of money and credit was crucial in an international trading centre like Bruges. Money-changers, bankers and other credit-providers were particularly important in the fourteenth century, which was constantly afflicted with inflation, speculation and currency debasement. The role of the money-changers, especially in the fourteenth century, cannot be overstated. They co-operated with the city's hoteliers to provide financial services to local, regional and international traders, from Prussia to Italy and Spain. They offered current accounts, deposits, money transfers and even banknotes (though only on a local basis), alongside more conventional money-changers operations, such as loans and investments in both the short and long term. The money-changers of fourteenth-century Bruges had, in fact, become bankers. Italian merchants settled their international monetary transactions using letters of exchange rather than cash. This inevitably created profitable business opportunities for Italian bankers. The trade was focused in Bruges around the square where the Genoese, Florentine and Venetian communities had their headquarters. It became known as the Beursplein, after the Van der Beurse family who ran a hotel there (now a branch of the Roeselare bank in Vlamingstraat). The term bourse to describe a stock exchange thus arose in fourteenth-century Bruges. Ordinary citizens who needed money were obliged to turn to pawnbrokers who charged extortionate rates of interest. The were known locally as lommerds as they traditionally came from Lombardy.

Bruges' money market thus had an international character, with an important contribution from native bankers and money-lenders. This was necessary because of the cosmopolitan nature of the overall city economy. Wool and sheepskins, lead and tin were imported from England and Scotland. Hides, wood, copper, dried and pickled fish, pitch and potash from the Baltic were offered for sale by the German Hansa. Wine was imported from France, the Rhine and Italy. The Iberian peninsula provided oranges and lemons, leather, wool, iron ore and sugar, while the Italians traded in luxury products, spices and other goods. Many of the imported products were processed in Bruges. The city was also the point of contact between the Mediterranean world (Italy, Spain and Portugal) and the north (Flanders, England and the Hanseatic League). The international presence in Bruges took on an added dimension towards the end of the fourteenth century with the dynastic fusion of the county of Flanders and the duchy of Burgundy.

The Town Hall that stands in Bruges to this day was built shortly before the beginning of the Burgundian period. Construction began in the final quarter of the fourteenth century (the first stone was laid in 1376), and reflected the supreme power enjoyed by the city at the time. The facade is a stylistic balance between the sober Gothic civic architecture of the fourteenth century and the exuberant late-Gothic of the fifteenth century. The Town Hall at Bruges clearly served as a model for other similar buildings in Flanders and Brabant, including the Town Hall at Leuven. Other surviving examples of fourteenth-century civil architecture consist primarily of traces left after later rebuilding. In 1974, for instance, monumental remains of fourteenth-century architecture were found in the facade of the house at Hoogstraat 36, enabling the original front to be reconstructed. The most striking fourteenth-century remains were found in 1994 at Spinolarei 2. The house itself probably dates from that period, but this is disguised by its prominent and much more recent stepped gable. Nevertheless, the interior contains fine fourteenth-century murals, including one of Saint George and the dragon and allegorical portrayals of the ten virtues. These were done some time between 1380 and 1400, their style and quality serving as examples of the pre-Eyckian realism that laid the foundations for the art of the Flemish Primitives in the Burgundian period.

Mediaeval Saint John's Hospital, 13th-century facade (Mariastraat)

HEROES OF 1302:
JAN BREYDEL AND PIETER DE CONINC

Bruges most famous statue stands in the Markt. It shows Jan Breydel and Pieter de Coninc, the city's heroes in 1302. The monument dates from 1887 and was designed by the Brussels sculptor Paul de Vigne (1843-1901). The base, which depicts a series of historical scenes and coats of arms, was produced by the local architect Louis Delacenserie (1838-1909). The unveiling of the monument was preceded by years of fund-raising, campaigning, string-pulling and fierce political controversy. When it was complete, it had to be unveiled twice, first by the liberal Breidel Committee on 11 July 1887 and then by the Municipal Breydel and De Coninck Committee on 15 August 1887. On the second occasion, both King Leopold II and Burgomaster A. Visart de Bocarmé gave speeches in French, which provoked immediate protest. Breydel and De Coninc were, after all, key figures in the vision of Flemish history promulgated by the Flemish Movement.

We ought to say something here about their historical role in the events of 1302. It is the local butcher, Jan Breydel, who most captured the popular imagination. He was born in around 1264 and died between 1328 and 1331. Breydel was captured by the French in 1301, together with Pieter de Coninc and 24 other resistance leaders, and freed shortly afterwards. On 1 May 1302, he helped lead a successful raid on the French garrison at Male. He was also one of the commanders on 18 May, during the events that came to be known as the Bruges Matins. He supplied William of Gulik's army with meat, horses and oats for the Kortrijk campaign, and after the Battle of the Golden Spurs he moved into the former home of a French sympathiser. He was given a number of profitable positions and was active in municipal politics, though without ever pushing himself to the fore. He was, however, involved in a number of violent incidents. A variety of surviving documents indicate that he was one of the most wealthy citizens of Bruges.

Pieter de Coninc, who was born between 1250 and 1260 and died in 1332 or January 1333, was a weaver of modest origins. He compensated for his shortness through his intelligence and his talent as an orator. De Coninc led resistance to the Francophile city council in 1301. He was subsequently imprisoned and released along with 25 others, and was clearly a ring-leader of the revolt. The sons of Count Guy of Dampierre clearly recognised him as such, sending De Coninc to Bruges, where he became undisputed leader in March 1302. He was forced to relinquish power in May, having lost the confidence of some of his supporters, but his authority was restored after the Bruges Matins and he duly helped the count's family lead the revolt against the French. He was knighted immediately after the Battle of the Golden Spurs, on 11 July 1302. Like Breydel, he moved into the former home of a French sympathiser. Although he did not occupy an official post, he continued to influence policy as a radical popular leader. In 1321, however, he chose the side of the count during a popular revolt, and was obliged to quit the city. In historical terms, Pieter de Coninc was a much more important figure than Jan Breydel.

HOSPITALS AND ALMSHOUSES. WELFARE INSTITUTIONS IN MEDIAEVAL BRUGES

Although Saint John's Hospital is discussed at length in several chapters of this book, it was far from the only welfare institution in and around Bruges. Most initiatives of this kind were not charitable in nature. They were organised instead by the city or by specific professions, to take care of colleagues in need. This is certainly the case with Saint John's, which was founded in the twelfth century and run by the city. Its purpose was to care for the sick and injured, and for travellers, all of whom were tended to by monks and nuns. The hospital was located in a four-hectare estate on the edge of the first ramparts, where it remained until 1976. The institution has since moved to modern premises in Sint-Pieters, leaving behind its impressive artistic legacy and historic buildings, which were duly transformed into a museum. It was entirely controlled by the city council until 1459, when the personnel adopted the Rule of Saint Augustine at the urging of the bishop of Tournai. The city council signed an agreement with the bishop in 1463, according to which the city remained responsible for the hospitals material affairs, while the bishop was to enjoy authority over the personnel, who were now monks and nuns. The former left the institution at the end of the sixteenth century. The sisters became marginalised in the second half of the twentieth century, as trained nurses began to dominate the hospital staff. These were employed by the city council once again and after 1976 by the OCMW (Social Services), making it the most recent successor to the mediaeval board of governors. Over the centuries, Saint John's developed from a nursing institution into a modern hospital offering advanced medical care in West Flanders. It has been regionally important throughout its history and the new Saint John's General Hospital continues to play this role for the north of West Flanders province, and parts of East Flanders and western Zealand Flanders.

There were other hospitals and hospices in mediaeval Bruges in addition to Saint John's, some of which survive to this day.

The Hospital for the Blind in Kreupelenstraat, for instance, was founded in the fourteenth century, originally for poor blind people. It developed into a almshouse for the elderly. The current set-up dates from the fourteenth century. Saint Justus Hospice in Ezelstraat was founded in the fourteenth century. Originally intended to provide temporary accommodation for the homeless, it was transformed in the sixteenth century into an almshouse for single elderly men. The Potterie Hospital at the end of Potterierei was even more important. It was founded in the thirteenth century and originally fulfilled the same purpose as Saint John's Hospital, although it was a great deal more modest in scale. Before the Middle Ages were out, the Potterie Hospital began to focus exclusively on caring for the elderly. The Potterie continues to operate as a home for pensioners to this day. The hospital's artistic heritage has been assembled in the sixteenth-century building adjacent to the three-aisled, fourteenth-century church.

The 46 almshouses spread around the town centre are a characteristic feature of the Bruges cityscape. They consist of a complex of pensioners' homes, some of them grouped around a communal garden, others in fine rows along the street, often with a chapel. A total of over seventy such complexes were built. Some were created as welfare facilities, aimed at elderly people from a specific profession. Others were founded as charitable acts by wealthy citizens. Most of the surviving almshouses are still used as homes for the aged, managed nowadays by Social Services. Some have been pressed into alternative use, the best known being the one founded by the Cobblers Guild. This seventeenth-century complex now serves as the Museum of Folklore in Balstraat. Bruges earliest almshouses were built in the fourteenth century. The most recent, the Moulaert house, was built in 1959 outside the old town, on the Blankenberg road in the Sint-Pieters district. Many almshouses have been restored by Social Services in recent years and adapted to contemporary requirements in terms of comfort and safety for the elderly. As a result, the number of homes per complex has often been reduced.

BURGUNDIAN BRUGES.
A GOLDEN CENTURY WITH AN ANTICLIMAX

Historians are rather ambivalent in their analysis of Bruges in the fifteenth century. Although the Burgundian town enjoyed obvious prosperity, the seeds of economic decline were, according to some historians, already in evidence. Bruges was clearly no longer the easily accessible port that had flowered in the high Middle Ages. Nevertheless, the silting of the river Zwin is no longer viewed as the principal cause of Bruges' decline, even though sea-going vessels had long been obliged to transfer their cargoes at Sluis. Smaller vessels then carried the merchandise via the canalised Zwin for sale in Bruges. The city had been granted staple privileges by the count in 1323, which meant that virtually all goods brought via the mouth of the Zwin had to be sold there. These privileges were secure in the first half of the fourteenth century, but Bruges was obliged to intervene in Sluis on several occasions in the fifteenth century to ensure compliance.

The traditional Flemish textile industry was also well in decline by this period. Flemish cloth had been the magnet that drew merchants from all over Europe to Bruges in the thirteenth century. They brought their own goods in exchange, for which they found a ready market in densely populated Flanders with its wealthy upper classes. They also came into contact there with many other merchants from all over Europe. Flemish cloth production began to experience intense competition in the fourteenth century from other, cheaper varieties of cloth, particularly from England and Holland. Even so, Bruges was able to retain its position as an international trading centre until the 1480s. The city's economy even experienced several important new stimuli towards the end of the fourteenth century. Half a decade of political unrest and military violence came to an end with the death of Count Louis of Male in 1384. He was succeeded by his daughter Margaret, who had married Philip the Bold, duke of Burgundy, in

Genoese Lodge of 1399 (left) and the inn run by the Van der Beurse family, with stone tablet dated 1453. Now in Vlamingstraat, this was the financial centre of the town until the 15th century

42
43

1369. So it was that in 1384, Flanders joined a group of territories between France and the German Empire, which were to develop into the Burgundian Netherlands. The merchants of Castile and Portugal were granted new trading privileges in Bruges in 1384, followed a year later by their counterparts from La Rochelle and Saint-Jean d'Angély. The Hanseatic League boycotted Flanders between 1388 and 1392, shifting their headquarters to Dordrecht in Holland. They returned to Bruges in 1392. The Genoese, who had long been based in England, came back in 1397. The city council provided them with a plot of land on the corner of Grauwwerkers-straat and Vlamingstraat, where the 'Genoese Lodge' was built in 1399, one of the few surviving foreign merchant headquarters. The facade has been considerably altered since the fifteenth century and many changes have been made to the interior. Nevertheless, the Genoese Lodge still has many indications of its original purpose. Restoration of the building was completed in 1983.

In other words, Bruges retained its place in the commercial first division in the fifteenth century, even though Antwerp and even Amsterdam were developing strongly at the time. Its population in 1477 is said to have been around 42,000, just as many as in the fourteenth century. Bruges' economy altered fundamentally in the course of the fifteenth century. Traditional cloth-making and selling declined and the city began to focus instead on a more diversified range of goods and services. Traditional products were replaced by high-quality luxury goods. Art, fashion, banking and finance became Bruges' principal economic activities. This process was accompanied by the growth of corporatism and quality control by specialist craft guilds, in which a growing body of highly trained craftsmen were organised. The Leuven historian Herman Van der Wee recounts that the most spectacular example of this process occurred in the artistic sector, where he took Flemish Primitive panelpainting as his model. The latter will be discussed at length in this chapter on the basis of important works of art in Bruges' museums. Other examples may be cited, too, such as the diamond trade, the armaments industry, miniature art, the production of luxury manuscripts and (from the 1470s) book printing.

Middle-class earnings grew strongly in Bruges (and in other towns in the Low Countries) in this period. Increased prosperity was attributable to the policy of monetary stabilisation pursued by the dukes of Burgundy, the lowering of food prices and higher wages for specialised labour. Local demand was another important contributory factor. Bruges' late-mediaeval municipal economy relied on strong local purchasing power and a highly developed network of merchants, brokers and bankers with contacts all over Europe. Without political stability, however, none of this could be sustained, and so the decade that followed the death of Duchess Mary of Burgundy in 1482 was to prove ruinous. The subsequent revolt against her widower, Maximilian of Austria, led to the collapse of Bruges's economy. Local prosperity evaporated to be replaced by a period of political instability, war and international isolation. The Burgundian court quit the city for good and Maximilian ordered the foreign merchants to leave as well. Most returned after 1492, but the rise of Antwerp as commercial metropolis had now begun in earnest and was to persist until around 1585. By 1494, Bruges found itself impoverished and depopulated. Between four and five thousand houses stood empty. Although the town was to achieve relative prosperity again in the sixteenth century, the golden years were never to return.

Bruges also had to contend with several other crises in the course of the fifteenth century. The most severe of these occurred between 1436 and 1438, when the town rebelled against Philip the Good, a revolt that the duke was to crush ruthlessly. He did not pardon the city until 1440. The duke had made peace with the king of France in 1435, causing England, the traditional enemy of the French, to suspend wool supplies to Flanders. Mounting tension between the French and English also led to military action against Flanders, which had an extremely adverse impact on Bruges. Trading relations between Flanders and England did not return to normal until 1439. In the same period, 1436-38, a dispute led the Hanseatic League to shift its trading headquarters from Bruges to Antwerp. All of these developments gave rise to an acute, albeit temporary, economic crisis in Bruges, which led in turn to famine

and an outbreak of plague. A second, though less severe, crisis
was sparked by Ghent's rebellion against Philip the Good in
1452-53. The revolt of Flanders' largest city against the duke
naturally had economic repercussions for the rest of the country,
including Bruges. The Hansa quit Bruges again in 1451-57, first
for Deventer, and later Utrecht, in response to a drawn-out dispute
with the duke. An Italian living in Bruges in 1452 translated a
Flemish chronicle into his native language, referring to the town
in his prologue as 'a living grave'. A third crisis broke out in 1477
on the death of Duke Charles the Bold. News of the duke's passing
sparked riots in Bruges. The new duchess, Mary of Burgundy,
and her advisors sought to contain the discontent, but were only
partially successful. The duchess was obliged to make a number of
concessions, and granted a new charter to the city. Bruges townspeople who had cooperated too readily with the Burgundian rulers
were swept from the political stage. The revolt against Maximilian
of Austria broke out five years later, in 1482. The conflict was to
drag on for years and resulted in the final decline of Bruges as an
international trading centre in the late fifteenth century. Despite these
successive crises in Bruges' history, we ought to stress once again
that the city experienced a golden age in the Burgundian period
(1384-1482). Visitors were fascinated by its economic vitality,
prosperity and luxury. Even today, tourists can hardly fail to be
impressed by the many surviving reminders of fifteenth-century
Bruges. We will take a look at the most important of these and
place them in their historical context.

The counts of Flanders gradually drifted away from Bruges in the
thirteenth century. In the fifteenth century, however, Bruges became
a capital once again, this time of the Burgundian Netherlands.
Reference to the Prinsenhof, which extended at the time from
Noordzandstraat to Moerstraat, was first made in a document
dating from 1396. It was the frequent residence of Philip the
Good (1419-1467) and his granddaughter Mary of Burgundy
(1477-1482). Duke Philip died at the Prinsenhof in Bruges on
15 June 1467, the city having been his favourite residence after
Brussels and Lille. Philip firmly established the aristocratic

Burgundian culture in Bruges. His successor, Charles the Bold (1467-77), whose reign was brought to an abrupt end by his death on the battlefield at Nancy, spent less time at the Prinsenhof, although his marriage to Margaret of York in 1468 was celebrated in Bruges. The wedding was marked by unprecedented festivity, with a lavish procession and tournament in the marketplace. The latter was called the Golden Tree tournament, a theme taken up by the organisers of the Golden Tree Procession, which was duly revived as a five-yearly event in 1958. Bruges remained the favoured residence of Charles' daughter and successor, Mary of Burgundy.

The cultural and artistic prestige evinced by the court of the 'Great Duke of the West' was undoubtedly felt more strongly in Bruges than elsewhere. The supreme example of this phenomenon was the painter Jan van Eyck, who had established himself in Bruges by 1430 and remained there until his death in 1441. Van Eyck was the first and greatest of the so-called 'Flemish Primitives'. He worked directly for the duke, and was thus exempt from membership of the local painters' corporation. It is evident, nevertheless, that he did not work exclusively for the ducal court. The city authorities paid him in 1434-35 for painting the statues at the Town Hall. He also worked for foreign merchants, members of the duke's entourage and his own friends and family. One of Jan Eyck's most famous panels is in Bruges' Groeninge Museum, Virgin and Child with Canon Joris van der Paele, Saint Donatian and Saint George. It is the largest surviving Van Eyck after the Lamb of God altarpiece in Ghent. We know much more than usual about the historical background of this painting. It was commissioned by Joris van der Paele, who might have been a native of Bruges. He became a canon at Saint Donatian's in 1387, but spent most of his time in Rome, where he was attached to the papal chancery. He settled permanently in Bruges in 1425 after a career in Rome lasting 35 years. He then led a quiet existence until his death in 1443, only fulfilling the very modest liturgical duties of a canon. He never became a priest and had no intellectual interests. He was, however, concerned about the salvation of his soul and the preservation of his memory. He thus arranged for daily masses to be said at his tomb in Saint Donatian's. For this to be done, he needed an altarpiece, and so in 1434 he ordered one from the illustrious Jan van Eyck. The brilliant painting was completed in 1436. Joris van der Paele himself is rendered so realistically that modern doctors have been able to identify the medical conditions from which the elderly canon suffered.

The second original Van Eyck in Bruges' Groeninge Museum is the portrait of his wife, Margaret. Van Eyck completed this small, intimate portrait on 15 June 1439. Margaret, who was 33 at the time, is presented as a rather cool, mature woman. The two paintings have never left Bruges since they were finished and have formed part of the city's cultural and historical heritage for centuries.

Virgin and Child with Canon Joris van der Paele, Saint Donatian and Saint John, panel painting by Jan van Eyck, 1436 (Bruges, Groeninge Museum)

No court painters of similar stature were active in Bruges after Jan van Eyck, but Petrus Christus, whose style was strongly influenced by his illustrious predecessor, became a citizen of Bruges in 1444. He might even have studied under Van Eyck, although all we know for certain is that he became a member of the city's guild of painters. His portrait of Duchess Isabella of Portugal, now in the Groeninge Museum, formed part of a triptych that was probably commissioned by the duchess herself. It is likely that Isabella was already living apart from her husband, Philip the Good, by the time the order was placed. Nevertheless, this panel, too, is redolent of Bruges' Burgundian past.

The third important artist in fifteenth-century Bruges whom we know by name was Hans Memling. He does not appear to have had any links with the Burgundian court, although twentieth-century romantics have vainly sought to identify the figures of Saint Catherine and Saint Barbara in his Triptych of Saint John as portraits of Mary of Burgundy and Margaret of York. The monumental painting, preserved in Saint John's Hospital in Bruges, is also referred to sometimes as the Mystic Marriage of Saint Catherine. Hans Memling became a citizen of Bruges in 1465, and died in the city in 1494. He received commissions from leading churchmen, Italian bankers, wealthy local and foreign townspeople and the monks and nuns of Saint John's Hospital. Although he never painted for the city authorities or the ducal court, he appears to have enjoyed some kind of patronage at the highest levels. This alone can explain why he was never obliged to join the painters' corporation, which was normally compulsory. Memling's most important 'Bruges' paintings are now displayed at the Memling Museum in Saint John's Hospital. The largest work is the Triptych of Saint John, to which we have already alluded.

As impressive thematically as it is in scale, the work was painted in 1474-79. The central panel shows the Virgin and Child enthroned, with Saints John the Baptist, Catherine, Barbara and John the Evangelist. Its composition was inspired by Van Eyck's Virgin and Child with Canon Van der Paele. The left part of the central panel and the left wing have scenes from the life of John the Baptist, while the right of the central panel and right wing have episodes from the life of Saint John the Evangelist. The details of the painting include

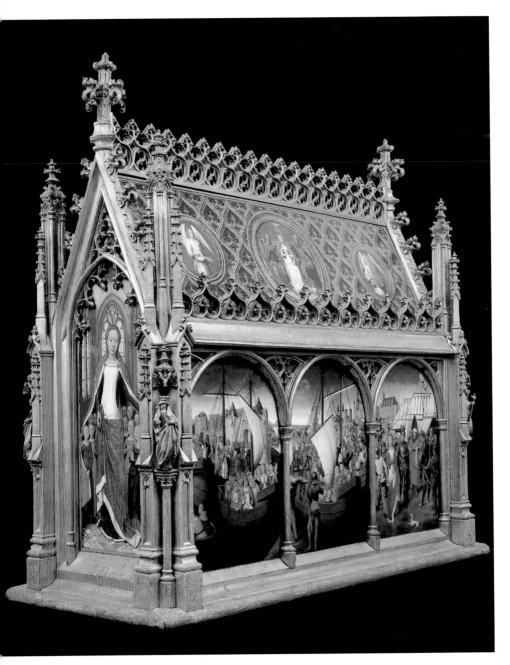

Hans Memling, *Saint Ursula Shrine*, painted in or before 1489
for Saint John's Hospital (Bruges, Memling Museum)

references to Saint John's Hospital. The triptych was commissioned by the four monks and nuns in charge of the hospital, who are shown with their respective patron saints on the outside of the wings. It was designed as an altarpiece for the hospital's high altar. Another important work by Memling that was commissioned by the hospital and has remained there ever since, is the reliquary known as the Saint Ursula Shrine. The wooden chest in the form of a late-Gothic chapel never held relics of Saint Ursula herself, but of the 'eleven thousand virgins' who, according to the legend, accompanied her on her pilgrimage to Rome and were martyred with her at Cologne. It was commissioned in 1489 to replace an earlier reliquary made in the fourteenth century, which has also survived. Like the Triptych of Saint John, it was commissioned by the hospital community, but on this occasion the donors are not portrayed. The shrine was kept in the hospital chapel and was used for centuries as a cult object. The six scenes represented on it narrate the pilgrimage and martyrdom of Saint Ursula and her companions. The narrow end shows her again with ten virgins, with the Virgin Mary and two of the hospital's nuns at the opposite end. The medallions on the 'roof' of the shrine were not painted by Memling. The figurines at the four corners might have been the patron saints of the donors. The work as a whole is redolent of the atmosphere that characterises all of Memling's works – modesty, serenity and refinement. The museums of Bruges have a significant number of paintings by Hans Memling and we do not have the room to discuss them all individually. It ought to be noted, however, that all the surviving Memlings in Bruges were produced for local clients. The same applies, incidentally, for most of the city's collection of Flemish Primitive paintings. A noteworthy exception is the panel showing the Death of the Virgin in the Groeninge Museum by the Ghent painter Hugo van der Goes. This impressive work, dating from around 1480, was probably commissioned for the Abbey of the Dunes in Koksijde. If so, the commissioner will have been Abbot Johannes Crabbe (1457-1488), who also ordered an altarpiece for his residence in Bruges from Hans Memling. The outsides of the wings of the latter work are to be seen in the Groeninge Museum.

The city's leading painter after Hans Memling was Gerard David, born in Oudewater in Holland. David became a free master in the Bruges painters' corporation in 1484. In 1515, he also enrolled in the painters' guild in Antwerp, typifying the situation in Bruges at the time. Nevertheless, David continued to work in Bruges, where he died in 1523. Two of his paintings are exhibited at the Groeninge Museum. The Baptism of Christ came from the Chapel of Saint Lawrence in Saint Basil's Church on the Burg, and was painted in around 1500. It is a modest, religiously inspired triptych. The Judgement of Cambyses, commissioned by the city council and finished in 1498, is very different. It is a shockingly realistic representation of a classical legend on the theme of justice. Its purpose was to remind the city's aldermen of their duty to dispense justice without fear or favour.

In addition to these artists whom we know by name, a great many anonymous artists were active in the fifteenth century. Most of them are known by general names, whereby their work is grouped on a stylistic basis around one key work. An example is the 'Master of the Saint Ursula Legend', an anonymous master who worked in Bruges in the final quarter of the fifteenth century, and became one of the city's most prolific artists. His work was influenced by known masters like Van der Weyden, Memling and Van der Goes, but he developed an individual style reminiscent of the miniature art of the Ghent-Bruges school in the same period. He owes his alias to a polyptych showing the legend of Saint Ursula and an allegory of the Church and the Synagogue in the Groeninge Museum. The legend of Saint Ursula and the eleven thousand virgins is recounted in eight small panels in greater detail than in Hans Memling's reliquary. The final panel shows a number of people worshipping at an altar devoted to Saint Ursula. The anonymous master successfully combined realism and spirituality in his work. The polyptych came from the convent of the Bruges Black Sisters – a community of pious women established in the mid-fourteenth century, which adopted the Rule of Saint Augustine in 1461. Throughout the fifteenth century, the nuns cared for the sick in their own homes. They did particularly valuable work during plague epidemics and other emergencies. It is unlikely that the nuns themselves could have afforded to commission the polyptych with the legend of Saint Ursula, although one of them might have been the model for the sister shown at prayer in the final panel. The scene gives much greater prominence to a number of lay people – probably Jan de Baenst and his family. De Baenst is known to have been a benefactor of the convent, and might well have presented the polyptych to it.

Jan III de Baenst was one of the most prominent figures in Burgundian Bruges. His wife, Margareta de Fever, had a similar background. Jan held a variety of posts in the city administration, including that of burgomaster on three occasions. He represented the city in various delegations from 1454 onwards, including the one to the Estates General, which was a kind of proto-parliament. First and foremost, however, De Baenst was a loyal servant of the Burgundian rulers, and so his activities were viewed much less positively by the ordinary citizens of Bruges. Their displeasure was shown in the spring of 1477 during the unrest that followed the death of Duke Charles the Bold. He was imprisoned on several occasions, together with other highly placed fellow townsmen, and accused of abusing his power. The events marked the end of his political career, but he remained an influential figure in the city. When Mary of Burgundy died in 1482, he unhesitatingly sided with her husband, Maximilian of Austria. His political allegiance obliged him to flee Bruges just before his death in 1486. His epitaph makes no reference to his posts in the city administration, extolling instead his services as an advisor to the dukes of Burgundy.
Jan de Baenst was the probable donor of the Saint Ursula polyptych. He is also known to have been an active patron of Middle Dutch literature in Bruges and to have been acquainted with William Caxton, the first English printer and a business relation of the Bruges printer and publisher Colard Mansion. His imposing home, now the Hof van Watervliet (Oude Burg 27), was built in the mid-fifteenth century. It was known at that time as the 'Hof van Sint-Joris', as De Baenst, who built it, was lord of Sint-Joris-ten-Distel (now a district in Beernem). When the building was restored in 1982, no fewer than eleven beautifully carved and painted corbel

pieces (auxiliary beams used to spread the load on a main beam) were discovered. The Hof van Watervliet is the only building with such a large number of original, painted corbel pieces from the fifteenth century. Several of them feature the emblem of the De Baenst family, while others include its coat of arms or the marital arms of Jan de Baenst and Margareta de Fever. In the sixteenth century, the house came into the possession of the Laurin family. Marc Laurin, lord of Watervliet and a leading Humanist, lived there from 1566. The current name of the building 'Hof van Watervliet', refers to its sixteenth-century residents.

The ducal court had an immense influence in the Burgundian period on the way of life of the upper classes in Bruges. The home of Jan de Baenst is a clear example of this. Much better known than De Baenst and the Hof van Watervliet, however, were Lodewijk van Gruuthuse and his mansion near Our Lady's Church, which nowadays houses the Gruuthuse Museum. Lodewijk van Gruuthuse, or Louis of Bruges as he is sometimes called, died in 1492 and is the subject of a special section in this book. All we will say about him here is that he was the foremost example of the profound influence Burgundian culture exerted on Bruges.

Jan de Baenst and Lodewijk van Gruuthuse were neighbours, living in the shadow of Our Lady's Church. Pieter Bladelin, meanwhile had an equally impressive home with a Gothic stepped tower in Naaldenstraat in the parish of Saint James, between the Prinsenhof and Beursplein. The building is now used as an old people's home. Pieter Bladelin (1410-1472) was about 26 when he was appointed municipal treasurer. He entered Philip the Good's service at the age of 30, managing the duke's finances and carrying out all kinds of political and diplomatic assignments. He used his own fortune to reclaim polders and to develop the town of Middelburg, now a peaceful little village in the municipality of Maldegem, roughly 20 km to the east of Bruges. He is famous throughout the world thanks to his portrait as donor in a Nativity by Rogier van der Weyden. The painting is now in Berlin, but was originally done for the church at Middelburg.

The Hof Bladelin was occupied in 1466 by a branch of the Florentine Medici bank, which was managed from 1473 by Tommaso Portinari. Portinari has gone down in art history as a client of Hans Memling and Hugo van der Goes. Like many other wealthy foreigners, he became fully integrated in the social life of the Burgundian-Flemish elite in Bruges. Portinari's admission into Burgundian circles was, however, destined to bring about his fall. Lorenzo de Medici terminated his association with Portinari in 1480, having become convinced that the Bruges banker had grown too closely associated with the highly risky financial policies of Duke Charles the Bold.

Portinari continued to work on his own account, but was ruined by the financial debacle that eventually engulfed the Burgundians. He was declared personally bankrupt in 1497. The Florentine occupation of the Hof Bladelin transformed the atmosphere of its courtyard into that of an early-Renaissance Italian palazzo, an impression that persists to this day. It is created primarily by the two medallions of Lorenzo de Medici and his wife Clarice Orsini, which date from 1469. Even without these ornaments, however, the Italianate inner courtyard is probably the earliest example of Renaissance architecture in the country.

Italians played an important part in the life of late-mediaeval Bruges. It was

Gruuthuse mansion, 15th century

Courtyard of the Hof Bladelin, Naaldenstraat,
the earliest example of Renaissance architecture in the country, 15th century

partly for this reason that the new cultural movements that arose in Italy were able to establish themselves there so quickly. Humanism and the Renaissance both appeared in Bruges in the fifteenth century, as opposed to the sixteenth in the rest of the Low Countries. Nor were they the preserve of foreigners. Lubert Hautscilt, abbot of Eekhout from 1394 to 1417, belonged to a cosmopolitan circle that included many Italians. He was probably one of the first Bruges people to read Italian Humanist texts. Half a century later, several clergymen had developed an interest in Italian Humanism. Evidence of this is supplied by the library of Abbot Johannes Crabbe of the Abbey of the Dunes, who spent most of his time in Bruges in this period. The Humanist influence is also clearly apparent in the work of Antonius Haneron (1400-1490), professor at Leuven, tutor to the young Charles the Bold, ducal diplomat and, finally, dean of the Chapter of Saint Donatian in Bruges. A variety of lay people also became acquainted with Italian culture. Printed books containing Humanist writings were available in Bruges from a very early date, even before book-printing became established in the city.

The Adornes family, originally from Genoa, had been fully integrated in the upper echelons of Bruges society since the fourteenth century. Several members were influenced in the fifteenth century by Italian Humanism. The family was involved in international trade and local politics. Like the De Baensts, the Adornes were intensely loyal to the Burgundian rulers in the fifteenth century. They are best known in Bruges as the founders of the Jerusalem Chapel, the adjacent mansion and the almshouses on the corner of Peperstraat and Balstraat, which date from 1471-83 (although the original foundation occurred in the second quarter of the fifteenth century). The chapel is particularly fascinating to visitors, its exotic architecture lending it an Oriental atmosphere. The complex has so far remained private, adding a touch of mystery that has visitors knocking on the door with a sense of trepidation. The chapel and adjoining buildings were built by Anselm Adornes (1424-1483). Like Jan de Baenst, Lodewijk van Gruuthuse and Pieter Bladelin, Anselm Adornes held important posts in the city administration. He was also a faithful servant of the dukes of Burgundy, on whose behalf he carried out a diplomatic mission to Scotland. While there, he won the confidence of King James III and was granted a Scottish title. He continued to visit the country regularly even after his political role in Bruges came to an end in 1477. He even became involved in Scottish politics and was eventually murdered there by a group of armed men on 23 January 1483.

Anselm Adornes features prominently in its interior. His monumental tomb, which he shared with his wife Margaret van der Banck, lies at its centre. It is Bruges' only surviving stone funeral monument from the fifteenth century. The two recumbent statues are powerfully and realistically executed and are well preserved. We also know the name of the artist who sculpted the monument. He was Cornelis Thielman, a local master stone-mason, who also worked on the remodelling of the Town Hall, the Prinsenhof, Saint James' Church and Damme Town Hall. Oddly enough, Anselm Adornes was not buried in the Jerusalem Chapel. Only his heart was brought back from Scotland and interred here. It is, however, the resting place

for most other members of his family. The chapel has tombs, commemorative plaques and funeral portraits from the fifteenth to the eighteenth century. The six stained-glass windows with portraits of members of the Adornes family and their patron saints, which date from 1560, are certainly worthy of mention. Together with the window of Jan IV de Baenst and Gertrude de Berlettes in Our Lady's Church, produced in around 1510-30, the windows in the Jerusalem Chapel are the earliest and most important example of stained-glass art in Bruges.

The architecture and interior of the chapel itself refer strongly to the Church of the Holy Sepulchre in Jerusalem. Pieter and Jacob Adornes, Anselm's father and uncle and the original founders of the chapel, are said to have made two journeys to

16th-century stained-glass window portraying Pieter Adornes and his wife Elisabeth Braderic (Jerusalem Chapel)

Palestine. Adoration of the Holy Places, especially Jerusalem, was a family tradition. Anselm Adornes and his son Jan also visited Jerusalem in 1470. The family displayed a modest piety, one manifestation of which was their special interest in the Carthusian Order. The influence of Italian Humanism on the family was equally important in terms of Bruges' cultural history. Pieter Adornes, Anselm's father, cherished the ambition of opening a public library in the Jerusalem Chapel along the lines of Cosimo de Medici's Florentine library of 1430. Anselm Adornes himself copied Humanist manuscripts. The Adornes read classical Latin literature, modern Italian Humanist authors and works on history and geography. They were one of the city's most cosmopolitan families in the fifteenth century and helped herald in the beginning of the Modern Age.

Escutcheons of the Knights of the Golden Fleece, 1478
(Choir, Holy Saviour's Cathedral)

LODEWIJK VAN GRUUTHUSE (c. 1427–1492)

Lodewijk van Gruuthuse or Louis of Bruges is the clearest example of the cultural 'Burgundicisation' of the upper classes in Bruges. He was the loyal vassal of successive Burgundian dukes for most of his life. The son of Jan IV van Gruuthuse and Margaretha van Steenhuyse, he inherited several important estates and fiefs in Flanders. He married Margaretha van Borsele of Zealand in 1455. Generations of his family had held the 'gruutrecht', a monopoly on the herbal mixture ('gruut') used to flavour beer. The privilege was substituted in 1380 by a tax on beer following the widespread replacement of this seasoning with hops. The 'gruuthuis' was the store in which the mixture was originally kept. It was transformed in the first half of the fifteenth century into a luxurious mansion for the family. The thoroughly restored building next to Our Lady's Church is now the home of the Gruuthuse Museum. Sadly, virtually nothing is left in Bruges of Lodewijk van Gruuthuse's extremely important library.

The Gruuthuse Museum seeks to perpetuate Lodewijk's memory, although the interior of the building no longer contains more than a few genuine traces from the fifteenth century. One feature that has survived is the oratory. Lodewijk van Gruuthuse was given permission by the church authorities in 1472 to built this private chapel which enabled him to follow services at Our Lady's from a vantage point in his own mansion. The oratory provides modern visitors to the Gruuthuse Museum with a glimpse of the most Burgundian church interior in Bruges.

A portrait of Lodewijk van Gruuthuse, attributed to the Master of the Court Portraits, may be seen in the museum. It shows him in middle age. There is no doubt as to the identity of the subject, as his motto 'Plus est en vous' and coat of arms appear in the original frame. Lodewijk van Gruuthuse is portrayed as a knight in the Order of the Golden Fleece, to which he was admitted in 1461. His membership of this highly exclusive group is evidence that Gruuthuse was one of the most prominent personalities in the Burgundian Netherlands. Lodewijk van Gruuthuse entered the service of Duke Philip the Good in 1445. He saw to it that Ghent did not receive any support from Bruges during its rebellion in 1452–53. He was knighted by the duke in 1453 on the battlefield at Gavere, where Ghent was finally defeated. Gruuthuse then undertook a variety of important diplomatic missions. He was Philip's stadtholder (governor) in Holland and Zealand from 1463 to 1477. It is also plain that he continued to serve the dynasty faithfully after Philip the Good's death in 1467 and his succession by Charles the Bold. The latter gave him both diplomatic and military assignments. Nevertheless, his loyalty was called into question in around 1470. He was granted an English title in 1472, thanks to his good relations with King Edward IV. Gruuthuse resigned as stadtholder following the unexpected death of Charles the Bold in 1477. He subsequently played an important role in Bruges once again, where he negotiated with the rebellious population on behalf of Duchess Mary of Burgundy, successfully lowering the political temperature. Mary made him her first chamberlain, but his loyalty was again questioned in 1481. It is not clear whether Gruuthuse had already begun to distance himself from Mary's husband, Maximilian of Austria. Whatever the case, he did not automatically support Maximilian after Mary's death in 1482, and actually spent three years in gaol beginning in 1485. Gruuthuse was freed in 1488 to negotiate the release of Maximilian, who had himself been imprisoned by rebels in Bruges. Henceforth, he no longer supported Maximilian, and steadily drifted towards the side of the rebellious city. He fell from grace irredeemably in 1491 and died eighteen months later, on 24 November 1492, at his Bruges residence. It is remarkable how closely Gruuthuse's biography parallels the history of Bruges in the Burgundian era.

THE BURGUNDIAN INTERIORS
OF HOLY SAVIOUR'S AND OUR LADY'S

Throughout the fifteenth century, work continued indefatigably on the construction and decoration of the city's various churches. Parish churches like Saint James', Saint Giles' and Saint Anne's were completed in this period. All manner of guilds and religious confraternities, not to mention private individuals, contributed to the abundant interior decoration of Bruges' churches. Clergy and certain confraternities, especially at collegiate churches like Saint Donatian's and Our Lady's, provided a rich liturgy, further enhanced by boys' choirs and professional musicians. Modern visitors can gain an idea of this important aspect of late-mediaeval culture at the frequent concerts of early church music held in the city and at certain religious services.
Most church interiors were fundamentally altered over the centuries, but many still house works of art from the fifteenth century. The choir-stalls at Holy Saviour's, for instance, date from the second quarter of that century. The thirty wooden misericords are jewels of late-mediaeval carving. The coats of arms of the knights of the Golden Fleece painted in 1478 still hang above them. The Chapel of the Sacred Cross has a fine fifteenth-century Passion altarpiece, although this small Brabant late-Gothic master-piece did not originate in the church, but was placed there in the nineteenth century. The oak doors of the Shoemakers' Chapel are original and feature Gothic woodcarving from the mid-fifteenth century. The city's cobblers, whose guild-house was in Steenstraat, established their chapel at Holy Saviour's in 1372. Their emblem, a crowned boot, features in both the chapel and at their head-quarters. Most of Holy Saviour's late-mediaeval art works are no longer in the church, however, having been transferred to the museum of Holy Saviour's Cathedral.
The artistic heritage of Our Lady's, by contrast, remains largely in situ. Visitors to Lodewijk van Gruuthuse's private oratory (1472) in the Gruuthuse Museum are given a view of the choir, with the tombs of Mary of Burgundy and Charles the Bold and the coats

of arms of the knights of the Golden Fleece who held a chapter meeting here in 1468. These features combine to make the choir of Our Lady's the most Burgundian church interior in Bruges, even though most of the works of art on view date from the sixteenth century.

The tombs of Duchess Mary of Burgundy and Duke Charles the Bold were only restored to their original position in 1982, following several years of archaeological study. The latter revealed the lead coffin of the duchess and the lead urn of her son, Philip the Fair, together with several beautifully painted tombs dating from the thirteenth and fourteenth century. The funeral monument of Mary of Burgundy was completed in 1502, twenty years after her death. It is one of the most impressive late-Gothic tombs in the whole of Europe. The sarcophagus itself is black marble. The sculpture is copper and was produced in Brabant. It was probably designed by Jan Borman of Brussels and cast by Renier van Tienen. The tomb of Charles the Bold, Mary's father, was commissioned by King Philip II half a century later, and was sculpted in Antwerp. Most tourists probably do not notice the stylistic differences between the two monuments and the fact that Charles the Bold's tomb is no longer late-Gothic. The Passion altarpiece by Barend van Orley and Marcus Gerards on the high altar was not begun until 1543 and completed in 1561. It was originally intended for the church built to house the tomb of Margaret of Austria, Mary of Burgundy's daughter, at the French town of Brou, but it never arrived there.

Several works of art from the Burgundian period at Our Lady's are located in the ambulatory. The most noteworthy are the oratory of Lodewijk van Gruuthuse, to which we have already referred, the tombs of Lodewijk I (1454) and Lodewijk II de Baenst (1496) and their wives, and the Lanchals Chapel, containing the tomb of Pieter Lanchals, a supporter of Maximilian who was killed by the townspeople in 1488 for his gross abuse of power. Gerard David's Transfiguration of Christ on Mount Tabor still has stylistic links with the Flemish Primitives, but dates from the first quarter of the sixteenth century. The wings, by Pieter Pourbus, date from 1573.

THE ORDER OF THE GOLDEN FLEECE

Philip the Good was the first duke of Burgundy to spend much of his time at Bruges' Prinsenhof. Consequently, several of the crucial political events of his reign occurred in Bruges, beginning with his Joyous Entry on 22 September 1419. Also worthy of note are his wedding with Isabella of Portugal in 1430, his reconciliation with Bruges following the 1440 rebellion, the assembly of the first Estates General at Bruges Town Hall in 1464 and his impressive funeral ceremony in 1467.

It was also in Bruges that Philip the Good founded the Order of the Golden Fleece in 1430 to mark his wedding with Isabella of Portugal. His aim was to bind members of the elite together. Admission into the Order was the highest honour available to the Burgundian nobility. It also featured prominently in the life of the Burgundian court and in the spectacles that were regularly mounted as propaganda for the duke and his policies. The Order drew its symbolism from the Greek Legend in which Jason slays the dragon and wins the Golden Fleece, a symbol of bravery. According to another, more risqué interpretation, the Golden Fleece was a reference to the pubic hair of a blonde mistress of the duke. This story of this 'Bruges lady' was first recorded by a sixteenth-century French historian and published in 1620.

Whatever the case, the Order of the Golden Fleece was extremely important from the outset. Its members were drawn from the highest nobility. The semi-religious chapter meetings, fifteen of which took place between 1431 and 1491, were ceremonial assemblies at which new knights were invested and those present publicly declared their allegiance to the duke. Three chapter meetings of the Golden Fleece were held in Bruges in the fifteenth century – at Saint Donatian's Church in 1432, Our Lady's in 1468 and Holy Saviour's in 1478. The knights sat in the choir stalls above which hung painted panels bearing their escutcheons, surrounded by the chain of the Order. The boards remained after the meeting, leaving Bruges with two complete fifteenth-century series of 29 coats of arms belonging to knights of the Golden Fleece, one in Our Lady's Church dating from 1468 and one in Holy Saviour's from 1478. They were executed by the court painter Pieter Coustens (Pierre Coustain). Similarly complete fifteenth-century series are only to be found in Ghent and Mechelen, although incomplete sets still exist in 's-Hertogenbosch and Saint-Omer. Whether or not coats of arms of this kind can be defined as art is open to debate, but they are undoubtedly examples of late-mediaeval craftsmanship of the highest standard.

SIXTEENTH CENTURY.
THE BEGINNING OF A NEW ERA

It is commonly believed that Bruges fell silent after 1500, declining economically, commercially and culturally to become merely a provincial centre. It is tempting to project back the image of decay portrayed in Georges Rodenbach's late-nineteenth-century novel *Bruges-la-Morte* over the entire period from the sixteenth century onwards. Bruges' decline was not so straightforward, however. Although the city had ceased to be the commercial hub of north-western Europe by the sixteenth century, it nevertheless managed to carve out an excellent niche in the new world economic order. The discovery and exploitation of the New World shifted the focus of international trade from the Mediterranean to the Atlantic. What's more, the Low Countries were an integral part of the first world empire to be governed centrally by a modern sovereign, Charles V (1500-1558). The region belonged to the Habsburg empire in the sixteenth century, together with Spanish, Austrian and Italian territories, the German (Holy Roman) Empire and the colonies of the New World. Bruges received the young emperor with great enthusiasm in 1515.

The stakes were high. Royal interference had caused foreign merchant communities to quit Bruges in favour of the growing commercial centre of Antwerp. Bruges vainly sought to turn the tide by pursuing an economic policy based on its traditional strengths: its link with the sea, its staple trade, based on the presence of foreign commercial missions, and a dynamic textile industry.

Venetian galleys entered the mouth of the Zwin for the last time in 1520, but access to Bruges' foreport of Sluis was becoming increasingly difficult. Sea-going vessels preferred to moor at Arnemuiden or Middelburg. Bruges spared neither effort nor expense to safeguard its link with the sea, and commissioned engineers to draw up plans for combating the silting of the Zwin and even

Pieter Pourbus, Portrait of Jan van Eyewerve, 1551 (Bruges, Groeninge Museum)

for making Bruges accessible to sea-going ships once again. The implementation of a series of plans, each more fantastic than the last, cost a fortune but consistently failed to solve the problem.

Despite these setbacks, Bruges managed to adjust to its new situation in the course of the sixteenth century. The presence of Bruges merchants at the annual markets of cities like Antwerp and Bergen-op-Zoom grew steadily, and the city's traders also mingled with their international counterparts at smaller ports on the western Scheldt. The mouth of the Scheldt functioned as a single entity, with ports like Middelburg and Arnemuiden substantially dependent on Bruges. The respective development of Bruges and the new commercial metropolis of Antwerp was thus complementary rather than competitive. Bruges merchants traded in spices and other colonial goods, and even in English cloth – all products that underpinned Antwerp's growth. Relatively speaking, it was still the leading commercial city in the Low Countries in 1569, although it had been entirely eclipsed in absolute terms. Antwerp became the undisputed commercial hub for the Atlantic community, its population passing the 100,000 mark in the sixteenth century, while that of Bruges levelled off at 30,000. The continued presence of Spanish merchants, who controlled by far the most important wool staple in the Low Countries, is a further indication that Bruges' importance did not simply collapse in the sixteenth century.

The Spanish trading community, which concentrated on the wool business, remained faithful to Bruges. Imports of light Spanish wool employed thousands of Flemish workers in the manufacture of light drapery. Members of leading Spanish merchant families, including the Pardos, de la Torres and Arandas, were well integrated in city life. Several of them took administrative posts and were granted prestigious estates in the surrounding countryside. Their daughters were married off to prominent local men, accompanied by substantial dowries, or were enthusiastically received by Flemish convents. The prosperity of the Spanish community is evident from the large buildings on Spanjaardstraat and the adjoining streets built in this period, many of which incorporate Renaissance features. The importance of Bruges as a centre of the wool trade grew even further when the English wool staple was transferred there from Calais in 1558. The Merchant Adventurers (English cloth traders) by contrast, chose Antwerp for their staple, and provided employment for dyers and other cloth-workers in a large area around the city.

Businessmen from Bruges itself continued to be involved in inter-national trade in the sixteenth century. Their companies focused on the Mediterranean and Baltic regions. The flexibility of the city's merchants is witnessed by the fact that the products in which they traded were not necessarily sold locally, but in Antwerp and elsewhere, too. The best known example of the dynamism of the Bruges merchant sector is the Compagnie Despars, which was founded at the end of the fifteenth century, but rose to prominence in a period when Bruges is popularly supposed to have been in economic free-fall. Bruges merchants continued to do just as much business with Portugal in the sixteenth century. The Mouscroun family and its agents were active in Italy in the early part of that century, and it was through Jan Mouscron that a marble Virgin and Child by Michelangelo found its way to Bruges in 1506, one of the few sculptures by the great Italian master to end up outside Italy. We also know of dozens of smaller companies (Wynckelman, De Boodt, Vanden Heede, etc.) whose interests lay in the Baltic region, from which they imported products like grain, tar and wood.

In other words, Bruges' commercial sector was sufficiently robust and flexible to hold its own in the changing world economy. In the

De la Torre House, Spanjaardstraat, 16th century

long term, however, it was destined to decline, as a result of which many of the city's merchant and entrepreneur families withdrew their capital from the risky field of trade and invested it instead in country estates and summer retreats. It is to these families that the city owes the wealth of chateaux and estates in the surrounding countryside. Bruges thus ceased to be the hub of an international system of distribution that underpinned a varied range of local industries. The evolution towards large enterprises that occurred in certain other European cities was destined to pass Bruges by. Population growth and urban development slowed to a halt, and there were no further ambitious building projects. Precise figures are not available, but the population may have stabilised around the 30,000 mark. A quarter of these people were living in poverty in 1544. The city council launched a series of initiatives to tackle the problem with varying degrees of success. In 1573, a 'Berg van Charitate' was founded. This institution, literally a 'mountain of charity', was a free lending bank, located on the Lange Rei in the seventeenth century (now nos. 7-11, the current home of the Land Registry).

The economic policy pursued by the city aldermen was geared towards restoring the local textile industry, traditionally the most important provider of employment. The sector had been caught by surprise by the immense international demand that grew up for light fabrics. Numerous attempts were made throughout the sixteenth century to initiate the production of light cloth or serge in Bruges. Only the serge-weavers of Hondschoot managed to create a lasting industry, as witnessed by the Saaihalle or 'Serge Hall', located in the former headquarters of the Genoese merchants. Better prospects were offered by the weaving of fustian from wool and cotton, production of which rose to 42,000 lengths a year by the mid-sixteenth century. Supply problems – cotton was a colonial product – caused the looms to fall silent on more than one occasion. Elements of the luxury industry continued to prosper in Bruges. The city remained a world centre of manuscript illumination until 1520, with the work of the miniaturist Simon Bening as its high-point. Wealthy aristocrats and merchants came to Bruges to order Books of Hours illuminated in the exuberant 'Ghent-Bruges' style:

Michelangelo's Madonna, a feature of Our Lady's Church since 1506

an attractive art form that continues to draw thousands of visitors to exhibitions organised all over the world. The work of the city's jewellers and carpet-weavers was equally fine, as witnessed by recent exhibitions in Bruges. What's more, Bruges continued to attract great master painters. Gerard David, who provided a link with the art of the Flemish Primitives, was followed by Jan Provoost, Adriaan Isenbrant, Ambrosius Benson and Pieter Pourbus, all of whom settled in Bruges. Pourbus in particular left behind an extensive oeuvre, many of his works remaining in Bruges' churches and museums. He was a Renaissance painter who devoted himself to a wide range of disciplines. He produced maps, altarpieces and portraits of the sixteenth-century Bruges elite.

The Italian influence on both the themes and execution of Bruges painting show how the Renaissance had taken root in this region. Bruges had passed its economic zenith by the late fifteenth and early sixteenth century, the period in which the Renaissance ideal was imported from Italy, which explains the sloth with which the new cultural influences made their appearance in the urban setting. A new architectural style was sought on the basis of traditional forms. Building continued in the Gothic style throughout the sixteenth and even into the seventeenth century, as a result of which Bruges is now possibly the most Gothic city in all Europe. The incorporation of window bays in a single, flowing gable-line had the effect of updating Bruges' typical Gothic house-fronts. Even so, the first Renaissance facades did begin to appear in the cityscape, albeit sporadically. The city's oldest surviving Renaissance front is that of the Oude Griffie, the former Recorder's House, on the Burg, which was built by the government in 1534-37. The citizens of Bruges were slow to adopt the Italianate style of construction. Several large houses owned by Spanish wool merchants in Spanjaardstraat were given additions inspired by the architecture of classical Antiquity, but the purest example is to be found at no. 33 Oude Burg (1571).

This reluctance to adopt Renaissance architectural styles was not matched, however, in the literary world of the Humanists. Erasmus of Rotterdam even called Bruges the *New Athens*. Although he tended to be rather bold in his pronouncements, Erasmus certainly visited the city frequently and looked forward to his encounters there with likeminded scholars. His regular host was Mark Laurin (1488-1540), dean of Saint Donatian's chapter, and the central figure in a network of Humanist friends and scholars in Bruges and many other European cities. Leading Humanists like Erasmus, Juan Luis Vives and Thomas More were particularly attracted to Laurin's house in Bruges by special occasions like the Ceremonial Entrance of Charles V (1515) and the reception given to Henry VIII of England (1521). Humanism in northern Europe differed from its Italian counterpart in its special focus on a purer religious life. It is no coincidence that the Abbey of the Dunes in the late fifteenth century and Saint Donatian's chapter in the sixteenth century came to be centres of renewal. It is typical of Bruges that links were also forged with the laymen who held important administrative and economic positions within the city. These included Frans van Cranevelt, city pensionary

between 1515 and 1521, and Cornelis van Baersdorp, who was burgomaster in the early 1560s. Such links help explain the 'enlightened' policies pursued in Bruges in an otherwise turbulent sixteenth century.

One progressive initiative on the part of the city authorities was the plan in 1517 to found a *Collegium Trilingue*, at which Latin, Greek and Hebrew were to be taught. The foundation of a similar institution in Leuven had been held up by the conservatism of the university authorities there. Bruges' college never got off the ground, but other centres of Humanist education were created.

Memorial bust of the Spanish-born Bruges Humanist Juan Luis Vives in the garden of the Gruuthuse Museum

Saint Donatian's chapter school began to teach Greek in 1518, followed ten years later by the chapter of Our Lady's. Bruges was thus home to several leading Humanist scholars, such as Adolf van Meetkerke, Peter and Bonaventura de Smedt (Vulcanius) and Pieter Nans. A *Collegium Bilingue* was opened by the council in 1540. One of the first Humanist teachers and lecturers to come to the city was Joris Cassander. The brevity of his time in Bruges (1541-43) was inversely proportional to his influence – Humanism here in the mid-sixteenth century was indisputably Cassandrian in character. Mark Laurin, nephew of the dean of Saint Donatian's, remodelled the Hof van Watervliet on the Oude Burg and was the central figure and patron of the city's Humanist circle. In 1558, he brought the brilliant printer and artist Hubertus Goltzius to the city, where he set up his workshop on Biskajersplaats. Thanks to Laurin's patronage, the Bruges intelligentsia were able for a time (1563-66) to publish in their own city.

The active involvement of the secular world in Bruges Humanism led to further enlightened initiatives. The practical ideas of the Spanish-born resident Juan Luis Vives in the fields of education and poor relief had an inspirational impact. The city council founded schools for less well-off children (the Bogarden School for boys in Katelijnestraat – now the Municipal Academy – in 1510, and the Elisabeth School for girls in Ezelstraat in 1518).

The emergence of Protestantism, which permanently shattered the unity of western Christianity, was one of the most pressing topics of conversation within Humanist circles. The Habsburg sovereigns Charles V and Philip II adopted the stance of resolute defenders of the Church of Rome. They were not prepared to concede an inch in their self-imposed mission. The city authorities in Bruges, however, took a more tolerant and pragmatic line, partly for fear that a repressive climate would drive away foreign merchants and businessmen. Lutheran and other heterodox literature was already circulating in Bruges shortly after 1517, when Martin Luther made his first public appearance in Wittenberg. Its readership consisted primarily of small groups which met in secret to read the Bible, some of which had contacts in Germany. Hendrik van Dommele belonged to one such group, and was eventually burned at the stake on the Burg in 1527, Bruges' first Protestant martyr. Seventy other people, mostly Anabaptists, were executed in the period up to 1572. The Anabaptists rejected the practice of baptising children and were the first to turn their back on the traditional church in order to form their own congregations. They tended to be people of modest means from all over the region, who lived in the poorest districts of Bruges. Their story is a fitful one, with the organisation of closely-knit, secret communities that constantly had to be dismantled.

Unlike the Anabaptists, the Reformed Protestants who began to gain ground from the 1550s onward, did not live on the margins of urban society. Calvinism established itself as Bruges' dominant Protestant movement thanks to strong organisation and discipline, links with

communities in London and Germany and an influence on the city's commercial sector and even the upper echelons of the city's administration. The Calvinist community presented itself in 1566 as a public opposition group that sought the allocation and recognition of its own places of worship. Protestants in most towns managed to achieve these goals, not least through a wave of image-breaking that left a trail of destruction across churches and monasteries. In Bruges, however, the narrow power-base of the local Protestant community and the resolution of the city council prevented an iconoclastic fury and any other public manifestation of the new worship within the city walls.

The 15th-century Hof van Watervliet, Oude Burg, home of Mark Laurin in the 16th century

The arrival of the duke of Alva (1567-73), who, with his Council of Troubles, established a climate of unprecedented repression in the Low Countries, brought the city of Bruges into painful confrontation with the centralist state. The resistance mounted by the city council succeeded primarily in protecting Bruges' own citizens. In any case, most religious dissidents had already fled to England and Germany in 1567-69, following which their remaining possessions were confiscated. One such refugee was Marcus Gheeraerts, who had shown himself to be a talented painter and engraver. In 1562, the city council had asked him to produce an exceptionally detailed plan of the city, reproductions of which still adorn a great many living room walls in Bruges.

The breakthrough of Protestantism was accompanied by reform within the traditional Church. So it was that the bishopric of Bruges was founded in May 1559, with the city itself as the bishop's seat. The move formed part of a policy designed to head off regional support for the Reformation. At the same time, Saint Donatian's became a cathedral chapter. The bishop recruited his closest collaborators from within the ranks of the newly appointed, university-educated canons. The deanship of Saint Donatian's was given to the bishop, which meant in concrete terms that the bishop and his administration moved into the deanery buildings on the Burg, which remained the episcopal residence until 1795. The privileged chapter of Saint Donatian, which for centuries had formed a city within the city, was slow to accept this development. Bishop and chapter were destined never to enjoy a harmonious relationship.
The elderly Pieter de Corte (Petrus Curtius, 1491-1567) was installed as the city's first bishop in 1562. A native of Bruges, with immense experience in the field of theology and the struggle against Protestantism, Curtius was obliged to work under difficult circumstances which prevented him from bringing about a religious turnaround. His successor, Remi Drieux (Remigius Driutius 1519-1594), faced similar problems. Little was done even in pressing areas such as the organisation of better training for priests. A seminary had been founded in 1571 at Ridderstraat 7 (Sint-Patriciushuis), but was closed again in 1578 when the

Calvinists took control of the city council. The current intake was obliged to finish its training at the Jesuit college.

The establishment of a Jesuit monastery and college in Bruges was exceptionally important to the spiritual and cultural climate of the city. The Jesuit Order was founded in 1534 by Ignatius of Loyola and rapidly developed into the principal Order of the Counter-Reformation. Bruges had a special significance to Ignatius, who had visited the city as a student on several occasions in around 1530 to seek the financial support of its Spanish merchants. The college opened in 1575 at the house known as 'De Lecke' on Sint-Jansplein (now the Hemelsdale Institute). The former Saint John's Church was adopted as its place of worship. The Jesuits returned to the city remarkably quickly after their expulsion during the Calvinist regime (1578-84), and took the opportunity of moving into larger premises on Sint-Maartensplein, where what is now Saint Walburga's parish church recalls their presence.

Strong anti-Spanish sentiment arose amongst various levels of the city population in the late sixteenth century. The roots of this feeling lay in the blatant interference of Spanish churchmen in city affairs, the reports they sent King Philip in his distant Escorial palace and the high-handed way in which Alva ignored the traditional privileges of the city and its inhabitants. These grievances were exacerbated by Spanish plans for financial reform, the garrisoning of Spanish soldiers and other unpopular measures. All this had led Bruges to take an active part in negotiations to achieve a consensus between the provinces (Pacification of Ghent, 1576). When the new governor, Don Juan, arrived in the Low Countries in 1577 and effortlessly crushed the armies of the rebellious Estates-General, fears arose of a new Spanish reign of terror. The subsequent anxiety pushed the cities into rebellion, although Bruges was not in the vanguard. To improve the city's defences, several large buildings just outside the city walls were demolished. This marked the end of Saint Catherine's Church (Assebroek), the Carthusian monastery of Genadedal (Sint-Kruis) and the convent of the Annunciation Sisters (just beyond the Ezelpoort). Churches, monasteries, convents, chapels and craft guilds also supplied gold and silverware to help meet military costs.

In Ghent, meanwhile, things went considerably further. Radical anti-Spanish citizens seized power in 1577-78. Apart from their opposition to Spain, they also wanted to restore Ghent's mediaeval hegemony over the rest of Flanders. On 20 March 1578, troops from Ghent entered Bruges, replaced the city council and set up a Revolutionary Committee (22-26 March 1578). The change of regime also gave Bruges Protestantism the opportunity to regroup. Petrus Plancius, for instance, was briefly active as a Calvinist preacher in the city in the spring of 1578. Protestants began to preach openly at Saint Anne's church in July and later in the churches of the Carmelite and Augustinian monasteries and in Saint John's Church. Anti-Catholic feeling began to spread, with the Jesuits and mendicants as the first target. The Franciscans in particular paid a heavy price. Three monks were publicly burned on 26 July having been accused of sodomy. Their remaining colleagues were expelled from the monastery or even the city, and their buildings were demolished. Jacob de Broucqsaulx, the Calvinist leader and burgomaster at the time purchased the superior's house, and a bleaching-works and timber market were built on the site of the monastery buildings at what is now Koningin Astridpark.

The recovery and breakthrough of Protestantism in Flanders and other regions undermined the remarkable unity that had arisen within the Low Countries in recent years. The territories controlled by the rebellious Estates joined in the Union of Utrecht, to which Bruges reluctantly added its name (1 February 1580). Protestantism was immediately given free reign, becoming the city's only recognised religion (24 May 1581). With the exception of the dismantled Saint Anne's, all parish churches were taken over by the Protestants between May 1580 and June 1581, and a school was attached to each one. Even so, the city's Reformation proceeded very slowly. Between 1578 and 1584, when Bruges was reconciled with Spain, it was primarily a part of the city's upper class who embraced Calvinism.

In the meantime, Catholic life had all but ceased in Bruges. Many of the city's monks, nuns and priests sought a new life further to the south, in cities like Douai and Lille. The churches were taken over by Protestant preachers, and the former monasteries and chapels were put to a wide range of uses. The Chapel of the Holy Blood, for instance, became the home of a 'public' library, and the site of the demolished Franciscan convent was used for a bleaching and dying works. Eekhout Abbey became a storehouse and a barracks for foreign troops, while the Carmelite convent of Sion remained intact but was pressed into service in the battle against the plague. Nevertheless, several smaller monastic communities were tolerated by the Protestant authorities, which meant that Catholicism was never entirely suppressed - another respect in which Bruges was unusual.

The region was forcibly reconciled with Spain in 1584 by the vigorous military and diplomatic campaigns of Alexander Farnese. The consequences were catastrophic. First and foremost, hundreds of dynamic individuals turned their back on Bruges and moved to the Protestant north, contributing enormously to Holland's subsequent Golden Age. Oddly, with the exception of Simon Stevin, virtually all these figures have been expunged from Bruges' municipal memory. Military operations continued after 1584, cutting Bruges off from the north. Even Sluis was dragged permanently from Bruges's sphere of influence. The countryside around the city was left fallow for many years. The fall of Antwerp in 1585 marked the permanent division of the Northern and Southern Netherlands and the closure to southern shipping of the vital river Scheldt. These setbacks were followed by an acute crisis that caused Bruges' economic life to contract disastrously in the final years of the sixteenth century. It was with a heavy heart that the elderly Zeger van Male penned a moving lament to the decline of his city. The close of the sixteenth century marked the end of Bruges' glorious history even more emphatically than the crisis of the late fifteenth century. Henceforth, the city was condemned to a provincial role, as the Dutch plied the world's oceans and set the intellectual tone throughout Europe.

SIMON STEVIN

Bruges and the Southern Netherlands were the clear losers in the sixteenth-century revolt against Spain. Merchants, scholars, artists and craftsmen all moved abroad. Many natives of the city helped build what was to become Holland's Golden Age. The most famous of Bruges' emigrants at this time was Simon Stevin, who featured in a list of the founders of Netherlandish civilisation drawn up by the authoritative Dutch historian and cultural philosopher Jan Romein. A square bearing Stevin's name was laid in Bruges in 1819, and a statue was installed there in 1847.

His merits as a scientist are well known, but we know little about his life. He was an illegitimate child born in Bruges in 1548, who soon found his way into the financial world. He began his career as a bookkeeper in Antwerp before becoming a tax official in Bruges in 1577. He then disappeared from his native city, possibly spending some time in one of the commercial towns in the Baltic. Stevin was in Leiden in 1581, where he studied at the newly founded university and came into contact with Prince Maurice of Nassau. Rather than pursuing an academic career, he threw in his lot with Maurice, first as tutor, and later as advisor and confidant. He died in Leiden or The Hague in 1620, leaving behind a young widow and a large family. Throughout his life, Simon Stevin styled himself Simon Stevin van Brugghe.

His work was highly versatile and practical. His guiding principal was always to pursue science with a useful goal in mind. Stevin was best known as a mathematician, but he also carried out pioneering research in countless disciplines: development of the decimal system, perspective, bookkeeping, navigation, astronomy, military and hydraulic engineering and others. These theoretical advances were matched by an endless series of practical achievements.

Another of Stevin's innovations was to publish most of his scientific work in Dutch at a time when Latin was still very much the language of scholarship. He was convinced of the power of his mother tongue, and gave it a new scientific vocabulary, much of which remains in use today. Words and concepts like 'in de oneindige' (to infinity), 'hoofdstuk' (chapter) and 'evenredigheid' (proportion) can be traced back to Stevin's desire to establish Dutch as a fully-fledged scientific language.

Simon Stevin's immense importance did not go unnoticed in his native Bruges. The Romantic movement in the nineteenth century determined to honour the great figures of the past. It was decided in 1841 to pay tribute to Stevin with a statue to be erected on the little square bearing his name that had been laid out in 1819 after the demolition of the Westvleeshuis in Steenstraat. Stevin's return to Bruges was not, however, destined to be a smooth one. In the first place, the figure of the great scientist provided material for political conflict. Traditional sections of Bruges society were outraged that a man they viewed as a *traitor* and *heretic* should be honoured in this way. The commission was finally given to the Liège artist Louis-Eugène Simonis. The statue was cast in bronze and shows Stevin standing with a pair of dividers in his right hand and his left hand resting on a manuscript. The inauguration ceremonies in July 1846 generated a week of Stevin fever in Bruges, even though the statue was not yet in place. Simonis did not complete the work on time, with the result that Stevin was only installed on his base on 9 September 1847.

PIETER POURBUS

Pieter Pourbus was Bruges' most important Renaissance artist in the second half of the sixteenth century. He was born in Gouda in around 1523 and came to Bruges at an early age. He married the daughter of the painter Lanceloot Blondeel and worked in the city until his death in 1584. His son found Bruges stifling and sought his fortune in Antwerp instead.

In the true Renaissance tradition, Pieter Pourbus achieved mastery of several disciplines. He was the painter of large altarpieces and portraits, a cartographer, architect and the designer of ceremonial decorations, funeral monuments, posters and seals. Most of his clients lived in Bruges and the surrounding area. Some twenty of his paintings remain in the city, making Pieter Pourbus its best represented Renaissance artist.

Once again, echoes of mediaeval art continue to reverberate strongly throughout Pourbus' oeuvre. His portraits in particular belong to a tradition stretching back to the Flemish Primitives. For that reason, he was often described in the nineteenth century as 'Bruges' last great painter', the man who rounded off the era of the Primitives. Above all else, however, Pourbus was an artist who mastered the innovations of Italian art, as witnessed by his monumental figures, his use of linear perspective and his Renaissance ornamentation. We are more or less certain that Pourbus never set foot in Italy. It seems increasingly likely, however, that he trained under Jan van Scorel, the artist and entrepreneur, who had set up a large and influential workshop in Haarlem in the 1530s after a prolonged stay in the cradle of the Renaissance.

Pourbus is best known for his portraits, a reputation perpetuated by his son Frans I and grandson Frans II. Bruges's social elite liked to be portrayed amongst the tokens and emblems of its elevated status.

Paintings of this kind were intended to be hung at home. The portraits of Jan van Eyewerve and his wife Jacquemyne in their house in Vlamingstraat (1551) marked Pourbus' artistic peak. The two matching works are to be seen in the city's Groeninge Museum.

Another impressive achievement was Pourbus' Map of the Liberty of Bruges, commissioned by the body that governed the area around but not including the city. A fragment of the map and a contemporary copy by Pieter Claeissens are displayed in the Municipal Archive in Bruges. The map was a real tour de force. It was the first time such a large painting (323 x 651 cm) had been done on canvas outside Italy, and clearly displays the artist's cartographic training.

Pieter Pourbus, Portrait of Jacquemyne Buuck, 1551 (Bruges, Groeninge Museum)

A MODEST TOWN
WITH A MARITIME VOCATION
(SEVENTEENTH AND EIGHTEENTH CENTURY)

The Southern Netherlands remained subject to the Spanish crown in the seventeenth century. Under the terms of the 1713 Treaty of Utrecht, however, the region became part of the Austrian empire. It was caught up throughout the period in the rivalry between the expansionist powers of France, the United Provinces (Holland) and Britain. These had developed an unfortunate tendency to fight out their military conflicts in what was to become Belgium, earning the region its tragic reputation as the Battlefield of Europe.

The countryside fared very badly in almost a century and a half of violence. For its part, Bruges came out of this period of military advances and retreats relatively unscathed, although it was occupied by the French in 1744-48. A strong defensive girdle was constructed around the town in the seventeenth century, when the mediaeval defences were converted into more modern fortifications. The old city gates were retained, however, and four of them still provide access to the city today (Ezelpoort, Smedenpoort, Gentpoort and Kruispoort). The inner defences comprised a series of bastions, while the outer fortification had both bastions and compressed earth ravelins, interspersed with stone constructions. They were not very effective and when the French military engineer Vauban visited the city shortly after 1700, he immediately proposed an updated set of fortifications. These never got beyond the drawing board. Bruges' city walls fell into disrepair in the course of the eighteenth century, and Emperor Joseph II finally ordered their dismantling between 1782 and 1784. Part of the inner wall was demolished, and the land underneath later used as a promenade surrounded by greenery. The old cross-section is still clearly visible between Boeveriepoort and Bevrijdingslaan, comprising a high inner wall, a wide moat, a lower outer wall and, finally, a narrower exterior moat. The boundaries marked out by the mediaeval city walls never came under pressure in this period. The city's population was slow to

Palace of the Liberty of Bruges, now the Administrative Centre on the Burg,
designed by the Amsterdam architect Jan Verkruys, 1721-27

recover after its decline in the late sixteenth century and numbered just over 27,000 inhabitants in 1620, rising to almost 38,000 by the end of the seventeenth century. Although this took Bruges back towards its fourteenth-century heyday, many other European cities had already passed the 100,000 mark. What's more, Bruges population slipped back again to just over 30,000 by the end of the eighteenth century.

There was little need, therefore, for new building, although there was a great deal of renovation and conversion. Most of the wooden frontages were replaced by stone in the course of the seventeenth and eighteenth century. The municipal authorities played a significant part in this process in the shape of new building regulations. Only two wooden facades now survive, at Genthof 7 and Korte Winkel-straat 90. Over 800 wooden frontages were demolished in this period and the town was given a new Baroque and Classical appearance. Some 500 eighteenth-century facades can still be seen in the town. Streets like Ridderstraat were almost entirely transformed. A series of majestic townhouses also appeared in the mid-eighteenth century, including the Hotel van Borssele (Sint-Jacobsstraat 23, now the City Conservatory) and the elegant house with its Rococo facade (Sint-Annarei 22) that dominates the view of the canals from Jan Van Eyckplein. Orangeries, like the one that survives in the backyard of Oude Burg 21 (visible from the bank of the Dijver) brought a touch of exoticism within reach of the wealthier burgher.

The new townhouses were evidence of a lively entrepreneurial spirit in the city. Bruges remained a port and commercial centre of western European importance in the seventeenth and eighteenth century, although many obstacles were placed in its way. The separation of the Northern and Southern Netherlands (the former becoming the United Provinces) led to the closure of the river Scheldt. In 1604, Bruges' mediaeval foreport of Sluis was lost to Holland. Large-scale investments were made in an attempt to devise an alternative route to the sea, whereby Antwerp and its Brabantine and Flemish hinterland would be linked to the modest North Sea port of Ostend. This development gave a powerful boost to Ostend, which had hitherto been a small fishing port. However, it also created new opportunities for Bruges, which was incorporated in the prestigious new network of canals. The town became accessible to small sea-going vessels from Ostend in 1622 thanks to the canalisation of the leperleet. Two other modest North Sea ports, Nieuwpoort and Dunkirk, were linked to the canal in later years. Bruges was also given a waterway leading to the river Lys at Ghent – the realisation of another mediaeval dream. An extensive hinterland was now linked by internal waterways to the North Sea via Bruges. Now that ships could reach Bruges via Ostend, the city underwent a revival as a sea port. This development took concrete form in 1664-65 with the excavation of a town dock near Dampoort, just outside the city walls where the canal left for Ostend. Maritime revival immediately breathed new life into the city's commercial exchange. Merchants and ship-owners no longer met outside the inn run by the Van der Beurse family, now rechristened the Oude Beurse (Old Bourse), but in the market hall on the Markt. The government even set up a Royal Chamber of Commerce in 1667, with national responsibilities including the organisation of overseas convoys. The institution was short-lived, however, as it rapidly came into conflict with the recently founded City Chamber of Commerce. Its foundation shows, nevertheless, that Bruges had found a new vocation as a centre of maritime commerce. More than three hundred new citizens were enrolled between 1664 and 1666. By the end of the seventeenth century, the population of Bruges had risen again to near the 40,000 level. This maritime revival was carefully nurtured. It was difficult to proceed further inland by waterway, as Bruges had to be traversed by canal from Dampoort and Minnewater, forcing ships to pass right through the town centre. Larger vessels from Ostend were thus obliged to transfer their cargoes to the smaller boats operated by Bruges skippers who then carried the goods to Ghent. Bruges was not prepared to give up its recently restored maritime status and protectionism triumphed over the general economic interest.

This did not prevent Bruges' commercial sector from retaining its international position. The Southern Netherlands still belonged to the

Spanish empire in the seventeenth century, which brought immense benefits to local merchants and entrepreneurs. The city's trading companies opened branches in Lisbon and Cadiz, and above all in Seville, the gateway to the New World. Bruges men like Maarten and Willem Lootens moved to Seville in search of adventure and profit. The trade with Spain and the colonies consisted primarily of light fabrics like linen, serge and lace, which were shipped in Ostend and Bruges. The fortunes made through this trade enabled Bruges merchants to enter the Spanish aristocracy. Others returned home to show off their wealth and power. One of them was Paolo Cobrysse who became burgomaster of Bruges after returning from Spain. He bought Rooigem château at Sint-Kruis and founded an almshouse that bears his name to this day. The opportunities created by the city's new town dock enabled a fully fledged Greenland company to dispatch annual convoys to hunt whales between 1664 and 1688. The hoop skirts worn by Bruges ladies in the late seventeenth century were shaped by baleen extracted from locally processed Greenland whales.

When the Southern Netherlands were ceded to Austria in 1713, the region lost its trading privileges with Spain and its colonies. The apparent ease with which Bruges businessmen adapted to the new situation says a great deal about their resilience. Ship-owners and merchants began to dispatch vessels to the East and West Indies. At the same time, the Austrian regime was sufficiently strong to challenge urban protectionism.

The maritime link with Ostend was deepened to allow sea-going vessels of up to 400 tons to reach Bruges. Every year, an average of two hundred merchant ships tied up at the town dock. This number almost doubled in periods of high economic activity. Smooth transit shipment inland was now assured by the excavation of the Coupure in 1753. This canal linked the deepened and widened Lange Rei and Sint-Annarei with the ring canal between Kruispoort and Gentpoort. The new works represented the most fundamental alteration to the cityscape since the Middle Ages. The Dominican monastery lost part of its garden and some of its buildings. Increased commercial activity in the second half of the eighteenth century necessitated the construction of new warehouses at the town dock (1757, 1772 and 1781) to ease the burden on the Waterhalle and the market halls in the city centre. The earliest wing has survived and was restored in 1981. The Waterhalle, which had been one of Bruges' principal landmarks, taking up the entire east side of the Markt, was demolished in 1787. Its removal formed part of an effort commenced in 1750, which sought to improve communications by systematically building modern, paved roads. The city's Chamber of Commerce had a hand in most of these initiatives.

The Chamber was not, however, up to the task of enabling Bruges to retain a firm foothold in world trade. It was badly run and was even challenged at the end of the eighteenth century by a dissident alternative (the Chambre Ardente). A national colonial company was founded under the name Oostendse Compagnie (1722-27). Bruges was sidelined because of the vigorous efforts of Antwerp businessmen who preferred Ostend as the fleet's home port. Although little Bruges capital was involved in the venture, the city became an important marketplace for the tea and other merchandise brought back from China and Bengal. A merchant naval college (Ecole d'Hydrographie) was opened in Bruges in 1781, but moved to Ostend barely five years later.

The maritime trade also breathed new life into Bruges industry, which was steadily developing away from its traditional craft base. Workshops for fine

Warehouse at the (old) Town Dock, Fort Lapin

faience and porcelain were set up in the second half of the eighteenth century by men like Pieter de Brouwere, who brought English craftsmen over from the Potteries and exported his goods to the West Indies. The De Brouwere family were a perfect example of Bruges businessmen with successful international ventures.

The rise of tobacco factories and sugar refineries was made possible by the import of colonial goods, but the city's biggest trump card remained the textile industry, which supported a quarter of its population. The era of Flemish woollens was, however, long gone and fustian, linen, serge and lace were now the main products.

In spite of all this economic activity, a substantial proportion of Bruges' population went hungry. Charitable initiatives mushroomed. Almost thirty almshouse complexes were founded or renewed in the seventeenth and eighteenth century. Most of these mediaeval-looking little houses still bear the names of their founders, like De Meulenaere (Nieuwe Gentweg 8-54), Van Peenen (Boeveriestraat 9-19) and De Vos (Noordstraat 4-14). Poor relief was not centralised and taken over by the city until the second half of the eighteenth century, earlier initiatives having come to nothing. The success of the latest project was due in no small part to the backing of the enlightened bishop, Felix Brenart, and a number of socially engaged priests.

The Church's activities in this field were only part of an exceptionally successful Catholic reformation in the city. During the seventeenth and eighteenth century, churches were built, the number of monasteries and convents doubled and lay piety was promoted by dozens of initiatives. Never before had Church and religion featured so prominently in people's daily lives. Visitors to Flanders in 1770-80 described the region as one of the most Catholic in Europe. This vigorous Catholic revival was fully supported by the central government, which played an important role in the appointment of bishops.

The city's greatest bishop in this period of revival and growth was Hendrik van Susteren (1716-1742), the Jesuit-educated son of an Amsterdam merchant. He was a flamboyant prelate who paraded through the streets in his luxuriously decorated coach. He was known for his sumptuous table and he purchased the attractive estate of

Rooigem, described as a miniature Versailles, in Sint-Kruis. In 1738, he acquired the crumbling Hof van Pittem in Heilige Geeststraat and had it converted into an episcopal seminary to realise his goal of providing solid training for the priesthood. These eighteenth-century buildings now make up the bishop's palace. Bishop van Susteren's majestic funeral monument was carved by the local sculptor Hendrik Pulincx and may be seen in Holy Saviour's Church.

The bishop's concern for ecclesiastical training is illustrative of the importance of the priesthood. Bruges boasted one priest for every two hundred inhabitants at this stage. Sunday Mass, sacramental life and the popular devotion that flourished in confraternities and processions were shared by the entire community. The Jesuits played a key role in the success of the Catholic Reformation. Following a less than promising start in the second half of the sixteenth century, they transformed Sint-

Maartensplein into a fully-fledged Jesuit quarter, with a monastery, college and Baroque church. The monastery church was designed by the Jesuit Pieter Huyssens between 1619 and 1643 and is easily the most important Baroque religious edifice in the city. The college was highly respected and their Sunday schools reached out to the lower classes, which mixed religious instruction with basic literacy. The Jesuit Order was suppressed in 1773 and the Baroque monastery church duly became Saint Walburga's parish church.

Saint Walburga's Church, originally the Jesuit's monastery church

The Jesuits were not the only success story. Bruges was transformed in the seventeenth and eighteenth century into a city of monasteries, even more so than during the Middle Ages. There were more than thirty new foundations, more than double the number in the previous period. Several new monastic Orders established communities in Bruges in the second half of the sixteenth century and above all after 1600, going on to play an important part in the Catholic reformation. The Jesuits were joined by Capuchin and Discalced Carmelite friars and sisters. Other Orders devoted themselves to education, founding schools that survive to this day. The Holy Family Institute is now a large school in Oude Zak, while the lace school near the Jerusalem Chapel was integrated in the Lace Centre in 1972.

The great abbeys in the countryside around Bruges transferred their activities to the city. They had all been badly scarred by the turbulence that marred the end of the sixteenth century. Monastic buil-

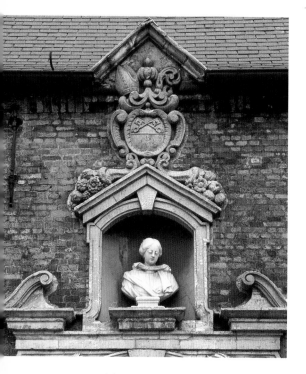

dings were destroyed and their communities scattered. The most important move was that of the prestigious Cistercian Abbey of the Dunes, which abandoned the ruins of its twelfth-century foundation in Koksijde to the encroaching sand. Its monks moved to Potterierei in 1627, occupying a refuge that had originally belonged to the Convent of Ter Doest in Lissewege. The latter had closed down and its property was inherited by the Abbey of the Dunes. An impressive new abbey complex was built under the inspirational leadership of Abbot Bernard Campmans (1628-42).

Godelieve Abbey, 17th century, Boeveriestraat

The church, with its strictly Classical architecture, was not completed until the eighteenth century. Since 1834, the well-preserved monastery buildings have been home to the Episcopal Seminary. Carthusian friars (Genadedal) and sisters (Sint-Anna-ter-Woestijne) also opted to live in the city. The Carthusians converted the former Saint Aubert's Hospital at the end of Langestraat into a new abbey. Its church has been successfully incorporated in the new courthouse built on the site of the former abbey in the 1970s. The best-preserved monastic building from this period is Godelieve Abbey in Boeveriestraat, which was occupied by Benedictine nuns who had abandoned their mediaeval foundation in Gistel.

The thousand or so monks and nuns who lived in the city can hardly be said to have played a dynamic role in urban life. What's more, the end of the eighteenth century brought a fairly abrupt end to this varied monastic life. The first blow was struck by Emperor Joseph II of Austria, who closed all monasteries without a social purpose in 1783. The communities that survived were then abolished in 1795 by the occupying French revolutionaries. The subsequent clearance produced open spaces that survive to this day. Koningin Astridpark and Sebrechtspark (Beenhouwersstraat – Oude Zak), for instance, were created by the demolition of the Franciscan monastery and the convent of the Grey Sisters (Saint Elizabeth's). A few communities, including that of Saint Godelieve's Abbey, survived the fury of the French occupation and reorganised in the nineteenth century, either at their original site or elsewhere.

The triumph of the Catholic Reformation demanded the sumptuous decoration of churches, chapels and monasteries. The interior of Saint Anne's Church in Bruges is a textbook example of Baroque art. It is a parish church, built in the early seventeenth century on the ruins of the mediaeval building destroyed during the Calvinist era.

Several generations of painters worked in Bruges for the local and regional market, overshadowed by the Baroque giants of Antwerp, like Rubens and Van Dyck. The seventeenth century was dominated by the Van Oost family. Jacob van Oost the Elder (1601-1671) trained in

Italy and then spent his entire working life in Bruges. His impressive oeuvre may be seen throughout the city, in most of its churches and in the municipal collection. His pupil Jan Baptist van Meunickxhoven (1620-1704) captured seventeenth-century Bruges in his painted cityscapes. The success of the Bruges school led to the foundation of an academy of fine art in 1717, which took up residence at the Poortersloge in 1720. The academy enjoyed its greatest success in the second half of the eighteenth century. Its directors at that time included Jan Garemijn (1712-1799), who remained faithful to Bruges throughout his life while becoming Flanders principal exponent of Rococo painting. Garemijn's landscapes, city views and salon pieces were snapped up by the social elite of eighteenth-century Bruges. The sculptors Pieter Pepers and Hendrik Pulinx also studied at the academy. Pepers' work is still visible all over the city, including the Rococo pump on the Eiermarkt (1761) and his impressive statue of Johannes Nepomucemus (1767) at the end of Wollestraat.

The final decades of the eighteenth century heralded in a new era. Ornamental Renaissance forms in Baroque and Rococo art gave way in around 1775 to the strictly classical style. European intellectual life, meanwhile, was being fundamentally renewed by the ideas of the Enlightenment.

The modernisation of the city's publishing industry typified the breakthrough of the new philosophy. Publishers, printers and book-sellers like Van Praet (in Kuipersstraat, now the Biekorf Library), Bogaert and De Busschere ran ornate bookshops, organised successful auctions and boasted that they could get hold of any book within a short space of time. Success was not slow in coming, as the libraries of the nobility, the entrepreneurial class and even the educated clergy were deemed incomplete without a good selection of the Philosophes. The administrative and ecclesiastical elite spoke fluent French, providing them with easy access to Rousseau, Voltaire and other enlightened spirits. French was also the working language of the Société Littéraire which was founded in 1786 as a meeting place for progressive elements in Bruges high society. The group provided the intellectual driving force behind the social changes that occurred at the end of the eighteenth century. It survived for two centuries and continues to play a modest role today as a French-speaking literary club.

Emperor Joseph II of Austria pursued enlightened policies in the Low Countries from the beginning of his reign. They initially provoked little resistance, even where religious reforms were concerned. We have already mentioned his abolition of monastic institutions that did not play a social role in education or health-care. He banned burials in and around churches in 1784 to improve public health, a measure that sounded the death-knell for inner-city graveyards, which are now recalled only by certain street-names (Sint-Gilliskerkhof, Sint-Salvators-kerkhof and Onze-Lieve-Vrouwekerkhof-Zuid). They were replaced by a central cemetery in Assebroek, which is still in use. A new cemetery called the Blauwe Toren was laid to the north of the city in 1976.

It was Joseph's attempts at political reform in 1787, however, that really provoked the opposition of the Church and traditional groupings such as the craft guilds and the dynasties that had grown up in the city council. The Brabant Revolution (1789-90) marked the end of Joseph II and saw the return of corporatism to towns like Bruges. The Austrian regimes attempts to claw back power were soon overwhelmed by the storms emanating from France after 1789. French revolutionary armies defeated the Austrians in 1792. They enjoyed a great deal of sympathy in Bruges. A Freedom Tree was planted in the marketplace, the carillon played the Marseillaise and the statues of the counts of Flanders on the Town Hall were symbolically smashed. The Société Littéraire was transformed into a progressive political club along the lines of the Jacobin club in Paris, and immediately set about establishing the revolutionary ideals of liberty, equality and fraternity in Bruges. The dismantling of centuries-old political structures resulted, however, in the collapse of urban society. The second French occupation, beginning on 25 June 1794 after a brief restoration of Austrian power, saw the eradication of the social order that had existed for hundreds of years. The foundations were laid instead for a new, modern society and the previous centuries were summed up dismissively as the *Ancien Régime*.

PALACE OF THE LIBERTY OF BRUGES

The Tourist Office and a number of other municipal services are currently based at the Municipal Administrative Centre on the eastern side of the Burg. The Centre is housed in the eighteenth-century buildings of the former Palace (Landhuis) of the Liberty of Bruges, on a site that was once the location of a residence of the counts of Flanders.

The development of the town had a great deal to do with the count's presence on the Burg. Their residence was the Steen on the western side of the square. A new, wooden residence was constructed on the opposite side of the Burg at a fairly early date, some time before the end of the eleventh century. It was later christened the Love after the covered gallery built against the facade. The counts preferred the comfortable Love to the cold, stone Steen, and it continued to be used as a residence until the fourteenth century, even when the other comital buildings on the Burg had been taken over by the municipal authorities. The construction of the Prinsenhof brought an end to the centuries-long presence of the counts on the Burg.

The newly released space was used by the council of the Liberty of Bruges. Also known as the Franc of Bruges, this was the name given to the countryside around the city. The district was a castellany, a territorial subdivision of the county. The Castellany of Bruges was created in around 1000, and ran inland from the North Sea coast – from the IJzer to the later Braakman at Biervliet – to Diksmuide, Torhout and Eeklo. The city of Bruges became a separate jurisdiction from the castellany in 1127. The Liberty of Bruges was not only Flanders largest castellany, it was also the wealthiest, which explains its presence at the assemblies of the Flemish Estates, the only rural territory alongside the towns of Bruges, Ghent and Ypres.

The administration of the Liberty of Bruges became steadily more onerous, causing its institutions to spread across the entire eastern side of the Burg. The derelict Love was partially rebuilt in 1520 and transformed into the Palace of the Liberty of Bruges. At the same time, the land to the south of the Love leading to Groene Rei was used for new construction.

The first buildings appeared between 1434 and 1440, and included the Vierschaar. The familiar municipal facades designed by Jan vanden Poele appeared on Steenhouwersdijk during an important cycle of construction between 1520 and 1525. The adjacent chapel dates from the early seventeenth century. Most of the rooms now form part of the Municipal Archive, although the council chamber is used as a museum.

This fine room, in which the aldermen of the Liberty of Bruges met for several centuries, is dominated by a monumental Renaissance chimney-breast. It was installed as a tribute to Charles V, possibly to mark the Treaty of Madrid (14 January 1526), in which Charles managed to extricate Flanders from its status as a French vassal. The chimney-breast is a masterpiece of early Netherlandish Renaissance art and was designed by Lanceloot Blondeel (1498-1561), a versatile artist who enlivened the city's cultural scene in the first half of the sixteenth century. It features the coats of arms of the 46 territories ruled by the emperor and life-size statues of Charles V himself and his four grandparents (Maximilian of Austria, Mary of Burgundy, Ferdinand of Aragon and Isabella of Castile). Combined visits can be made to the Renaissance Chamber of the Liberty of Bruges and the Gothic Chamber of the adjacent Town Hall.

It was decided in 1721 to rebuild the former Love. Spacious, Classical buildings were constructed (1722-27) from designs by the Brussels-based Dutch architect Jan Verkruijs. The sober, eighteenth-century architecture still dominates the eastern side of the Burg.

The French occupation marked the end of the *Ancien Régime*. The Liberty of Bruges ceased to exist as an administrative unit, and was incorporated in the new structures which have largely survived to this day. The abandoned buildings were put to new use as a law court. The courts recently moved to a new building at Kruispoort having dispensed justice at the Burg for two centuries.

The spacious complex was re-opened on 1 June 1988 as the Administrative Centre. Ten municipal departments are now housed there. The modern Burg is more than ever the administrative heart of the town. The finest chamber in the Centre, with its walls dressed in Cordoba leather, is currently used by the Tourist Office.

SAINT WALBURGA'S CHURCH

Saint Walburga's Church is the most impressive Baroque building in Bruges. Now a parish church, it originally served the Jesuit monastery. The imposing western front is on Sint-Maartensplein and is reminiscent of the Gesù Church in Rome. Bruges' Jesuit Church bears witness to the immense influence of the Order on the Catholic Reformation in the seventeenth and eighteenth century.

The Jesuit Order (Society of Jesus) was founded in 1540 by Ignatius Loyola and rapidly became a powerful religious movement with bases all over the world. The first Jesuits arrived in Bruges in the 1560s. Bishop Michel Drieux gave them a number of houses in Sint-Jansplaats (now Hemelsdale school) in 1574. By the end of the sixteenth century, the city's Jesuits were already in need of larger premises, which they duly found at Schottenplaats (now Sint-Maartensplein). They took possession in 1595 of the Hof van Moeskroen, a large mansion, and went on to take over the entire block as far as Verwersdijk, including the spacious Ireland and Scotland houses, and Schoofstraat. They built a monastery, a church and a college.

Construction of the Baroque monastery church began in June 1619. The architect was Pieter Huyssens, son of a Bruges stonemason, who had become a lay Jesuit brother at the age of twenty. Huyssens designed churches in Maastricht, Ghent, Namur and Antwerp (Carolus Borromaeus Church). By the time the institution was consecrated in 1642 and dedicated to Saint Francis Xavier, Huyssens had already been dead for five years. The architecture is fairly sober, but the church serves as a particularly fine example of the Baroque places of worship built in the Low Countries during the Counter-Reformation. The grandiose western facade is particularly impressive, while the interior stands out for its unusually wide central aisle and its relative restraint. Sandstone was preferred to marble. The church fittings provide a fine survey of seventeenth-century Baroque religious art. It clearly shows that Antwerp was the indisputable artistic centre at the time. One of the loveliest pulpits in Flanders was carved by the Antwerp sculptor Artus Quellinus the Younger (1670), while the two side-altars are by another Antwerp artist, Pieter Verbruggen (1657, 1669). Jacob Cocx, who made the high altar, also came from the city on the Scheldt.

The Jesuits were particularly well known for their work in the field of education. They pursued the same system in all countries, which placed great emphasis on self-study. Bruges' Jesuit college was not a very large institution, with no more than two or three hundred pupils. Courses lasted for five years, culminating in the rhetoric class. The school buildings in Boomgaardstraat have survived and were used as a state school for many years following the suppression of the Order.

The Jesuit Order was abolished all over the world in 1773, under pressure from European absolutist monarchs. It was not long before the Jesuits' church in Bruges was given a new role as parish church of Saint Walburga's (1779). The original, mediaeval Saint Walburga's Church was located nearby, on the corner of Sint-Walburgastraat and Ridderstraat. It was demolished in 1781.

Saint Walburga's was turned into a Temple of Law during the French occupation, but was restored to its parish function in 1804, although now under the name Saint Donatian's, which it bore for half a century. The real Saint Donatian's had, of course, been demolished by the French. The Jesuits returned to Bruges in 1840, following the restoration of the Order. Their current monastery in Korte Winkel was occupied in 1869. The original Neo-Gothic monastery church (1880-85) in Vlamingstraat has been used as a theatre for some years.

A POOR TOWN IN AN IMPOVERISHED FLANDERS, 1795-1895

The invasion of the Southern Netherlands by French revolutionary troops was followed by annexation on 1 October 1795. The citizens of Bruges were transformed at a stroke into citoyens of France, but it was to take a while for the new political culture to become established. It was two years before the installation of the first elected city council. Bruges also became the focus of a new judicial hierarchy and of the departmental and later provincial administration. The new structures laid the foundations for today's municipal and provincial institutions. Young radicals, who had first partaken of the revolution in Lille or Paris, brought extra dynamism to the new offices. The remaining posts were filled by French immigrants. Pierre Scourion († 1835) from Boulogne, for instance, was appointed municipal secretary, librarian and archivist in the early nineteenth century.

Throughout two decades of French rule, the region was buffeted by the gales of European politics. The French period came to an end in 1815, with the defeat of Napoleon Bonaparte at Waterloo. The Southern Netherlands were united with the North, to form the United Kingdom of the Netherlands, ruled by King William I of Orange. Bruges was far from pleased with its new sovereign. Although he did not try to reverse the advances made by the French in the field of municipal autonomy and administration, William was seen as a Dutch and Protestant monarch. His innovative policies in the fields of language and education generated a great deal of mistrust and were only supported by a small, Orangist group within the town. The Koninklijk Atheneum, the oldest secondary school in the town, was founded by William I. Bruges did not demur, therefore, when the revolt of 1830 led to the foundation of an independent kingdom of Belgium. When news of the Belgian Revolution was received in Bruges, the people's first response was to plunder the home of J.A. Sandelin, leader of the city's Orangist faction and the embodiment of fifteen years of Dutch rule. Bruges' 'renewed' municipal council was elected in early September

Side view of Saint John's Hospital in the painting Secret Reflet
by Fernand Khnopff, 1910 (Bruges, Groeninge Museum).
Khnopff illustrated the novel Bruges-la-Morte (1892)

1830, with Jan Baptist Coppieters 't Wallant as burgomaster. Coppieters represented the wealthy rural aristocracy and was an arch-conservative. Unlike many other cities, not a single Orangist retained a place on Bruges' city council. On 18 July 1831, Leopold I was given a very warm reception in Bruges as he travelled from London to Brussels. Three days later, he was sworn in under the new constitution as the first King of the Belgians. In the space of less than half a century, seven new flags had been hoisted at Bruges Town Hall.

French domination brought about fundamental political renewal in the region. When it came to shaping our modern world, however, the First Industrial Revolution had a much greater impact than any new institutions or ideologies. The wave of industrial renewal began in England at the end of the eighteenth century. Within a hundred years, little Belgium was to grow into a great economic power, the world's second industrialised nation. The First Industrial Revolution between 1790 and 1850, brought about an astonishingly high level of production and technology in the coal-mines, iron foundries and textile manufacturers of Wallonia. The mechanisation of the Ghent cotton industry in the early years of the nineteenth century, extended the industrial revolution to Flanders. The process was financed by the Brussels banks and the Société Générale. Antwerp made significant advances towards the end of Dutch rule, laying claim to much of the trade carried on via the river Scheldt, while commercial interests in Holland looked on with severe displeasure.

Bruges watched all of this from the sidelines, in spite of the fact that it held a number of aces that would have enabled it to industrialise its cotton sector. First and foremost, it had three centuries of experience in the production of semi-cotton fabrics (fustian). Bruges also boasted numerous cotton-printing works in the late eighteenth century. The city's Marlier family even found a way of printing in several colours and was operating over fifty looms on the eve of the industrial revolution. Profits from cotton printing led Ghent to invest in mechanised spinning and weaving mills, transforming the town into the leading Flemish industrial centre. Bruges' entrepreneurs, by contrast, refused to accept these risks, continuing to operate instead as merchants with a diverse range of interests. This led to a revival in port activities in the Dutch period. It is no coincidence that Jan Baptist de Lescluze, the most important ship-owner at the time, was the son of a fustian merchant. The family fortune was not invested in an industrial company, but in a trading venture. De Lescluze's ships plied the world's oceans, from Java and the Antilles to Saint Petersburg and the Levant. His preference, as chairman of the Ostend-based Chamber of Levant Trade, was for the Middle East. He was a personal friend of the Sultan of Turkey, and caused a great stir in 1824 when he exhibited an Egyptian mummy in Bruges.

The industrial revolution thus passed Bruges almost entirely by. Not one mechanised textile firm was set up. The crisis in the linen industry created an army of unemployed, transforming Bruges into the poorest town in the country by the middle of the nineteenth century. The long-standing economic focus on cottage industry was to prove

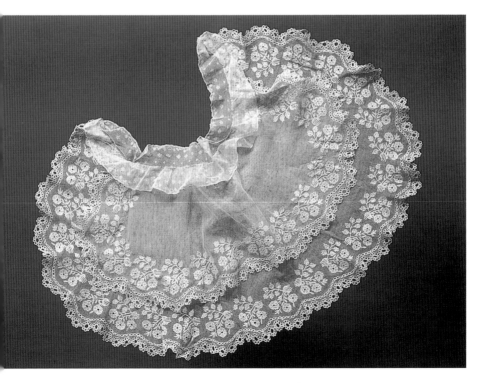

19th-century Bruges lace. Lacemaking was a typical cottage industry in the impoverished town (Bruges, Municipal Museums)

disastrous. Thousands of flax-spinners and weavers in the linen industry and almost ten thousand home-based lacemakers worked long hours for starvation wages. Lace schools were incorporated in the Christian charity network, where little girls were given free lacemaking lessons, but were not paid for what they produced, even though it was sold for a high price. Time-served lacemakers, who were entirely dependent on lace-sellers, did not do much better. The Dujardin bank, a family business with its roots in the previous century, and the city's only financial institution of any significance, was fittingly located in what was then known as the Vlasmarkt ('Flax Market' – now Garenmarkt), where the province's farmers came to do business. The bank's investments were concentrated in the rural sector. When they began to shift into industry in the 1870s, Dujardin's fell into difficulty. The failure of the bank ruined many small businessmen, and created a mistrust of the financial world that persisted in Bruges until the twentieth century.

The collapse of the linen industry and high food prices in the crisis years of 1845-50 hit Bruges very hard. The flight from the land created unprecedented demographic pressure. The city's population rose from 39,000 on the eve of Belgian independence to 50,000 in 1850. Forty percent lived in poverty, unemployment was never higher, and typhoid and cholera were almost daily killers. In the spring of 1847, gangs of starving citizens plundered bakeries and granaries. Large-scale soup distribution and the issue of bread coupons alleviated the worst of the privations. Bruges' hunger riots heralded in an exceptionally turbulent year in Belgian politics.

Major employment projects were planned, but never got off the ground. The Grossé brothers built a silk-weaving factory and silkworm farm at Ezelpoort on land provided by the city council. On the other side of the city, the banker Felix Dujardin set up two mechanised cotton-mills, one in Witte Leertouwersstraat and the other at Gentpoort, just outside the city walls. After ten years of operation, the latter employed two hundred workers. When the bank failed in 1874, however, the curtain also came down on this modest attempt at industrialisation in Bruges.

A positive turn occurred in the second half of the nineteenth century. Cottage industry continued to sustain most rural families, including three thousand lacemakers at the end of the century. The foundation of a variety of new businesses after 1880 created a more varied economic profile, although they remained small family and craft-type firms like blacksmiths, printing workshops, distilleries and breweries. Bleaching plants and horticultural businesses found the space they needed on the uninhabited areas on the edge of the town. The same period, however, also saw the creation of several successful enterprises that were to shape Bruges' socio-economic climate in the twentieth century: the De Jaeghere iron-foundry (renamed 'La Brugeoise' in 1905), the Verstraete distillery (which became the 'Nederlandsche Gist- en Spiritusfabriek' in 1895/97) and the Sint-Augustinus printing works on Houtkaai (1877) which belonged to the Desclee-De Brouwer family. The absence of large factories and an industrial proletariat also explains the limited success enjoyed by the labour movement in the town. A small Socialist nucleus formed at the end of the nineteenth century at the Spaans Heester tavern in Pottenmakersstraat. The co-operative bakery 'Werkerswelzijn' and a Socialist healthcare fund were set up in 1887, but Socialism in Bruges had to rely on the support of its big brother in Ghent until the eve of the First World War.

Although Bruges completely missed the boat during the First Industrial Revolution, the effects of industrialisation soon made themselves felt. The Ghent-Bruges-Ostend railway line was opened in 1838 – one of the first in the country and hence on the European mainland. The line entered Bruges via the uninhabited, low-lying grasslands (known as 'Meersen' and recalled today in the streetnames 'Oostmeers' and 'Westmeers') and followed the route of what is now Hoefijzerlaan. The first station was built on the Zand in 1844, but soon proved inadequate for the rapid growth in rail traffic. It was dismantled in 1879 and rebuilt in Ronse. Bruges' new Neo-Gothic station with its 'modern' iron entrance hall, was opened seven years later. The Capuchin monastery on the Zand was demolished to create the necessary space, but the important role played by the friars in populous West Bruges ensured that a replacement was built for them in Boeveriestraat. The prestigious building was demolished in turn in 1948 to make way for the current station and the construction of railway lines around the city. The Zand became a public square once again, and the old railway and marshalling yard were replaced by Koning Albertlaan and the adjacent park.

Bruges' true vocation, however, remained that of a sea-port. Napoleon toyed for years with the idea of linking Bruges to the western arm of the Scheldt via a canal through Damme, Sluis and Breskens. Planners worked vainly on similar projects in the fifteenth century and sixteenth. Once again, nothing was to come of the bold scheme. The ground was ceremonially broken in 1811, and Sluis was reached seven years later in the time of William I. That, however, was as far as it went, as the economic need for the canal evaporated on Belgian independence. What was left was a regular barge-service between Bruges and Sluis. The Damse Vaart (or Napoleon Canal, as it is sometimes called) has since established itself as one of the most characteristic landscapes in Flanders.

Within Bruges itself, however, the French Revolution left deep scars in the cityscape. The anticlericalism of the French led to the destruction of numerous mediaeval churches and monasteries. The gravest example was the demolition of Saint Donatian's Church on the Burg, which had been the very incarnation of the Ancien Régime. The process was long and drawn out, and Bruges entered the nineteenth century to the sound of sledgehammers smashing the church-bells, which echoed throughout the city. It was still possible, ten years later, for the children to climb the piles of rubble at Saint Donatian's to catch a glimpse of Napoleon and Marie-Louise's ceremonial reception in Bruges. All that now remains are the foundations of the twelfth-century choir, excavated in 1987-88, which can be seen in the cellars of the Burg Hotel. The large space freed up in the heart of the town was going to be transformed into a classical 'Place de la Préfecture' inspired by the Place des Martyrs or Place Royale in Brussels. The project never advanced beyond the laying of a square lined with plane trees, a road linking the Burg with Philipstockstraat and the conversion (1806-08) of the deserted bishop's palace into a stately residence for the prefect, and after 1830 the provincial governor.

This was not the only new building in the town. In 1820-21, the municipal architect Jan-Robert Calloigne built a classical-style, covered colonnade on Braamberg, the location of the fishmarket since the eighteenth century. It is the only important public building in Bruges dating from the period of Dutch rule. A concert hall, now De Korre Theatre, was built in Sint-Jacobsstraat in 1830. The fact that Bruges was the administrative capital of West Flanders was apparent from the eastern side of the Markt. In 1850, the provincial authority moved into the central part of the imposing Neo-Classical buildings that had replaced the Waterhalle at the end of the eighteenth century. The current Provincial Hall was not built until 1892.

Living conditions a short distance from the fashionable main streets were exceptionally poor, and slum-clearance was urgently needed. Hopes were raised when a Liberal burgomaster called Jules Boyaval took office in 1854, pushing the landed gentry aside in favour of the more enlightened bourgeoisie. The Liberal city council planned a new urban structure with wide, straight avenues. Most of its ambitious plans remained on the drawing-board, however, although one or two smaller projects were implemented.
The clearance of the theatre district, near the old Beursplein, began in 1864, prompted by the construction of the new concert hall to replace the hundred-year-old Comedie. The mediaeval street pattern disappeared entirely, and stately townhouses arose along the new, straight Adriaen Willaertstraat, Jacob van Ooststraat and Niklaas Desparsstraat, centred around the impressive new concert hall. It is the only part of Bruges that recalls the appearance of more dynamic nineteenth-century centres like Brussels and Lille.

The real Bruges survived in the west of the city, cut off from the centre by the Zand and the railway. The city council cleared the entire district to the west of Boeveriestraat. A core of small, unhealthy dwellings was demolished to make way for new streets and more spacious houses. Once again, speculation went hand in hand with the improvement of living conditions. Nothing was done about the slums in the parishes of Sint-Anna, Sint-Gillis and Sint-Magdalena and in the Meersen. These districts were dominated by poverty and unemployment, and typhoid and cholera outbreaks were common. It was here, too, that the pressure exerted by the growing population was absorbed. Landowners divided their gardens into plots and built one-room dwellings which they then rented out. The yards were closed off from the street by little gateways. There were still forty of these 'forts' as they were called at the end of the nineteenth century. The Wevershof, Fort Lillo in Verbrand Nieuwland and the streetname 'Sentillehof' near Gentpoortvest are reminders of these workers' dwellings. Most of the thousand plus public houses in the city were located in these working-class districts, a few minutes walk from the large inns and hotels on the Zand and the town centre. Roughly one house in seven was a drinking establishment. The many working-class bars in Langestraat are a legacy of that period. Langestraat's reputation as a night spot also owed much to the proximity of two large barracks – those of the infantry at Kazernevest since 1744 and those of the cavalry at the former Carthusian monastery in Langestraat after 1835/36. The barracks were demolished in the 1980s, leaving behind the monastery buildings, and the land used for the new law courts and a social housing project.

Bruges was a sleepy town in which life stood still and every building exhaled the breath of centuries. Perhaps it was this unusual atmosphere that attracted so many wealthy British families to move there. People rightly talked in the nineteenth century of an English colony that numbered 1,200 members at its 1869 height. It boasted its own schools, banks, shops, tea-clubs and an Anglican church (now the Jozef Ryelandt Hall in Ezelstraat). Nevertheless, it was primarily English Catholics who were drawn to Bruges.

Aristocratic families placed their children in the private school run by the English Convent in Carmersstraat, or in one of the many other little schools. The English Catholic convert and philanthropist Sir John Sutton supported an English Seminary from 1859 until his death in 1873, where both British and Flemish young men were trained to develop the Catholic Church over the Channel. Guido Gezelle was its deputy principal for a while, and taught philosophy.

British intellectuals left their greatest mark on the cultural and artistic life of nineteenth-century Bruges. William Edwards, the first librarian of the Ecole Centrale (1796-1808), the forerunner of the modern City Library, came to Bruges with his parents as a small boy, following a failed colonial adventure in Jamaica. The foundations of the city's print collection were laid by a gift from John Steinmetz, an internationally renowned collector who had settled in Bruges in 1819. The architect and mural painter William C. Brangwyn also spent many years in Bruges, where he collaborated with Thomas Harper King on the religious and historical wall-panels in the Chapel of the Holy Blood. His son Frank was born in the town in 1867, and later donated a large collection of his artistic work in 1936, forming the basis of what is now the Brangwyn Museum. It was James Weale, however, an irascible and versatile man, who was to have the greatest influence, through his tireless efforts in the study and re-evaluation of Bruges' artistic heritage. His research into early art (the Van Eyck brothers, Petrus Christus and, above all, Hans Memling) paved the way for the modern academic approach with which we are familiar today.

In 1865, Weale and a group of friends created the Société archéologique, with the goal of founding a collection of antiquities. Felix Bethune, Guido Gezelle and Karel Verschelde were also amongst the founder members. Temporary accommodation in the Gentpoort and Belfry was followed by a permanent home at the former palace of the lords of Gruuthuse, which the city purchased in 1874 to house the collection. The Gruuthuse Museum has since become one of the city's main tourist attractions.
Having gained its museum, the association turned its attention to organising special exhibitions. In 1867, the Société archéologique helped stage an exhibition of mediaeval Christian art. The dyna-mism of James Weale meant that the section devoted to Flemish Primitive art became an immense success and one of the most remarkable artistic events ever seen in nineteenth-century Belgium. A professional, academically sound approach is still the trademark of the successful, large-scale exhibitions organised by the municipal museums today.

The leading figures of English Bruges were closely linked with the Gothic Revival that spread from England to the rest of Europe in the nineteenth century. The Neo-Gothic style looked to the Gothic forms of the Middle Ages, but was characterised above all by a wholly Catholic, nostalgic atmosphere. Bruges thus became the ideal seedbed for the theoreticians, architects and decorative artists of the Neo-Gothic. The key figure was Thomas Harper King, a pupil of August Pugin, who enjoyed the support of the bishop of Bruges, Jean-Baptiste Malou. He drafted the plans for the new Magdalene Church which was built in the Neo-Gothic style between 1851 and 1853. The stained-glass workshop of Malou's cousin, Jean Bethune, became the beating heart of the Neo-Gothic movement in Belgium. It was only in the final quarter of the nineteenth century that the city council began to show an interest in the 'Neo' styles. A Catholic council returned to power in 1876, headed by Amedée Visart de Bocarmé. In addition to campaigning for a new sea-port (Brugge Zeehaven), the cornerstone of municipal policy became the development of tourism, with the goal of transforming Bruges into a Belgian Nuremberg. This entailed the beautification of the old town through the careful conservation and restoration of important historical buildings and the construction of new buildings in neo-Bruges styles. The municipal architect, Louis Delacenserie (1870-92), was heavily influenced by the French architect Violet-le-Duc. He was responsible in this period for the restoration of the Gruuthuse palace, the Tolhuis, the Poortersloge and the Chapel of the Holy Blood. Several major new projects: the Minnewater Clinic, the Provincial Court and the State Teacher Training College – were built in the neo-Bruges style. Municipal subsidies were introduced in 1877 to finance proper conservation of monuments.

The success of Neo-Gothic architecture in Bruges was accompanied by a vigorous revival of Catholicism. The bishopric of Bruges was re-established in 1834 and immediately set about restoring the immense damage wrought in the course of the past half century. French revolutionary politics had suppressed the Church after 1797, and Catholic policies were equally unwelcome in Bruges during the reign of the Protestant King William I. The absence of industrialisation and proletarianisation combined with the vigour of successive bishops to transform Bruges into Belgium's Catholic bulwark. The Church was so strong in Bruges that it suffered little practical hindrance from the separation of Church and State specified in the Belgian constitution. Bishops like Jean-Baptiste Malou (1848-64) and Joseph Faict (1864-94) were authoritarian figures who strongly resisted Liberal policies and founded or supported numerous Catholic charitable and social organisations.

The foundation and support of episcopal colleges was another focus of the battle between Catholics and Liberals. The freedom of education envisaged in the Belgian constitution led the Church to aspire to a homogeneous network of Catholic education. Sint-Lodewijk College was founded at the former Abbey of the Dunes in 1834, and soon became part of a network of over ten episcopal colleges in West Flanders. The college moved to Noordzandstraat (the present Zilverpand shopping centre) in 1846, and finally moved out of the old town to Sint-Andries in 1972. The college's commercial department became the independent Sint-Leo College in 1890, located at the Carmersbrug over the Potterierei, where the Carmelite Convent had stood until the French occupation. Episcopal colleges formed the ideal recruitment ground for new priests.

Training for the priesthood was organised at the Episcopal Seminary, which was also located at the former Abbey of the Dunes after 1833. The tireless energy and immense organisational skills of a great many priests ensured the Church's presence in every field of city life. Charles Carton (1802-1863) is best known as the founder in 1836 of a school for deaf and blind children in the former Spermalie Abbey in Snaggaardstraat. At the same time, he founded a community of nuns devoted to teaching and nursing. The Spermalie Institute (MPI) remains active today in the care and education of visually and hearing-impaired people. Carton was the founder-chairman in 1839 of the historical association called the Société d'Emulation, which is still the leading body of its kind in Bruges and West Flanders, enjoying an international reputation. He published and collected books, supported the Neo-Gothic movement and enjoyed a central role in the social, cultural and artistic renewal that occurred in the mid-nineteenth century through his efforts as a promoter of the Neo-Gothic movement.

Carton placed his extensive library at the disposal of the young Guido Gezelle (1830-1899), whom he encouraged in his early career as a poet.

The priest Gezelle was a much greater proponent than Carton of the West Flemish school, which cherished the ideal of a Catholic and rural society. His brilliant pen was gratefully deployed by his superiors in the battle to restore this vision of the past. Gezelle worked as a teacher, parish priest, poet, journalist and linguist and his restless energy underpinned the foundation of the journals 'Loquela', 'Rond den Heerd' and 'Biekorf'. Only the latter was to survive, continuing to this day to enjoy the respect of the historical and ethnographic communities with its characteristically Gezellian interests. Gezelle the poet helped give birth to modern poetry in Dutch and his works are still anthologised both north and south of the border. The house in which he was born in Rolweg has been converted into a Gezelle Museum, while his manuscripts and library are preserved at De Biekorf Municipal Library.

The work and influence of an important Dutch-speaking poet like Guido Gezelle ought not to blind us to the fact that the city's elite had adopted French as its cultural and social language by the end of the eighteenth century. The dominance of the French language was further reinforced by two decades of French occupation. The efforts of King William I to restore the position of Dutch in the administrative and educational fields were entirely reversed after 1830. By the mid-nineteenth century, French had become the language of politics and education, and the favoured medium of communication in the artistic, business and private lives of the nobility, higher clergy and bourgeoisie. To writers like Georges Rodenbach, Paris was the artistic and literary Mecca, and it was thus in French poetry and prose that he chose to reveal his petrified Bruges to the world. Rodenbach's refined artistry and melancholy reached their peak in the novel *Bruges-la-Morte*. Published in 1892 with a cover illustration by Fernand Khnopff, it enjoyed immense success. *Bruges-la-Morte* is more than a book. It is an attitude of mind that is still frequently adopted when writers attempt to capture the atmosphere of slumbering, nineteenth-century Bruges.

House of Guido Gezelle's birth in Rolweg, now the Gezelle Museum

GUIDO GEZELLE (1830-1899)

Guido Gezelle was undoubtedly the most important nineteenth-century poet writing in Dutch. He is still widely studied and read. Gezelle was born in Bruges on 1 May 1830. His father was a gardener who lived with his wife and five children in the Sint-Anna parish on the rural edge of the town centre. He attended primary school in Bruges and secondary school in Roeselare. He then trained for the priesthood at the Grootseminarie in Bruges (1850-54). His first years as a clergyman were very eventful and set the tone for his later life and work. He returned to the school in Roeselare between 1857 and 1859 to teach poetry, during which time, he had a life-long influence on pupils like Eugeen van Oye, Gustaaf and Hugo Verriest and Karel de Gheldere. He also produced his most original poetry in this period.

Throughout his life, Gezelle was the willing tool of authoritarian bishops. He returned to Bruges in 1860 to take up a teaching post linked to the British mission. He then served as parish priest in Saint Walburga's parish between 1865 and 1872. Although the priest's role was supposedly to care for the souls of his flock, the bishop was keen to deploy Gezelle in the intense ideological struggle that raged at the time. He single-handedly published 't Jaer 30 and 't Jaer 70 (1864-72) – polemical publications aimed at the ordinary man in the service of the Church. The turbulence of politics wore Gezelle out, and he was transferred to Kortrijk in 1872 to serve as parish priest. He took a long time to adapt, but matured into a productive poet who duly gained the recognition of the literary and academic world. The little priest became a founder-member of the Flemish Academy of Language and Literature and was awarded an honorary doctorate by the Catholic University of Leuven. Later honours were gradually to take on the character of mass spectacles. In 1899, the bishop of Bruges finally took him away from Kortrijk and appointed him rector of the English Convent in Bruges, near the house of his birth. Having come full circle, he died a few months later, on 27 November 1899.

Gezelle was in the thick of the changes that occurred in the nineteenth century through his work as priest, teacher, poet, publicist, journalist, translator, philologist and promoter of the Neo-Gothic movement. The body of writing he left behind is immense in both scale and quality. Gezelle was intensively involved with language throughout his life. His passionate interest in early Flemish culminated in his cataloguing of around 150,000 words, phrases and proverbs from the regional dialect. This work was supported by colleagues and friends he had inspired. Gezelle drew on this work for his poetry and his many articles in 'Loquela', 'Biekorf', and 'Rond den Heerd', journals which he founded or nurtured.

Much of Gezelle's life and work may be understood in terms of the nineteenth-century drive to achieve a Catholic revival. The rise of a modern, industrial society shattered the ideal image of a Christian, rural Flanders. The policies pursued by the bishops of Bruges were designed to restore Christianity in the region. Gezelle understood this mission perfectly and devoted his life to it. An awareness of nature and admiration for God's creation is always present in his poetry and he turned to the traditional Flemish language to express these feelings. He found his building blocks in the predominantly religious literature produced in the vernacular since the Middle Ages. Paradoxically, Gezelle's traditional philosophy was expressed via poetry that broke with established literary and cultural conventions.

The house at the end of Rolweg, has functioned as a Gezelle Museum since 1926. There are other reminders of the life of the poet-priest in Bruges. All the addresses at which he lived have been marked with commemorative plaques. A statue of Gezelle was unveiled in 1930 in the shadow of Our Lady's Church, some way from the quiet Gezelle Quarter. It was the final work of the sculptor Jules Lagae.

LACE

Bruges and lace are inextricably linked. Visitors to the town centre cannot fail to notice the many little lace shops. There are also many examples of historic lace in the city's museums, especially the Arentshuis Municipal Museum of Lace. The Lace Centre in the Sint-Anna district, away from the busy centre (Peperstraat 30, next to the Jerusalem Chapel), promotes lace by mounting exhibitions, publishing books and co-ordinating the local teaching of lace-making. People of all ages, from Bruges and all over the world, come here to learn the art of bobbin lace.

Lace can best be described as an open-work fabric, made with needle and thread or bobbins of yarn. The two principal types are thus called 'needlepoint' and 'bobbin lace'. Bruges is best known for the latter.

It is tempting to credit Bruges with the invention of lace, but there is no conclusive evidence to support this. Very little is actually known about the earliest origins of lace. What is certain, however, is that prominent townspeople were using lace-trimmed linen in the late sixteenth century. Jacob de Heere, for instance, a canon of Saint Donatian's is recorded as owning several lace handkerchiefs in 1578. The use of lace in the clothing of the sixteenth-century social elite can also be seen in the paintings of Pieter Pourbus. Indeed, a tour of the Groeninge Museum offers a fascinating glimpse of the development of lace in fashion throughout the ages. The seven-teenth-century Portrait of a Bruges family by Jacob van Oost tells us that flat lace collars were fashionable at the time, while the lace flounces hanging from the sleeves of the little girls painted by Matthias de Visch were popular in the eighteenth century.

Lace has always been a luxury product. It was not only used in the clothing of fashionable ladies and gentlemen, but also in priests' robes, church linen and fine household linen. The elite status of its consumers contrasted sharply with the terrible conditions in which it was produced in the slums of Bruges. The lace industry first arose in the city in the sixteenth century, but grew explosively in the nineteenth. The First Industrial Revolution passed Bruges by and cottage industries remained the norm. Some 6,000 women and girls were already employed in lacemaking by 1801, and the figure rose to 10,086 out of a total population of 45,000 in 1840. The number declined towards the end of the nineteenth century to just above 3,000. The lace industry disappeared from the Bruges economy in the twentieth century, certainly after the Second World War.

In the nineteenth century, however, lacemakers working in the open air were a familiar sight in the poor areas of town. They were mostly pieceworkers, relying on buyers who operated on behalf of the big manufacturers. Their meagre wages were barely enough to support their large families and so criminality and prostitution were common in the lace industry in periods of crisis.

Man's collar in Early-Flemish bobbin lace or Van Dyck lace, first half 17th century (Bruges, Arentshuis, Lace Museum)

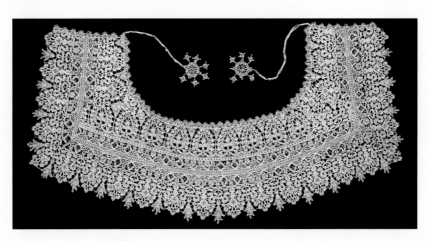

Bruges City of Museums, poster by Flori Van Acker, 1911.

BRUGES 1895-1970
AN AMBITIOUS PROVINCIAL TOWN

The novels of Georges Rodenbach paint a portrait of Bruges in the nineteenth century, but by the time they were published, in around 1895, the city was already on the threshold of the twentieth century. This marked the beginning of a period of very favourable economic development in Belgium, which came to be known as the Second Industrial Revolution. In the political sphere, general male suffrage (albeit with additional votes for qualified electors) was introduced in 1894. Although only a half-measure, it nevertheless served to broaden the base of bourgeois democracy. The first modest social legislation was passed and the Flemish Movement began to win its first victories.

It is against this background that we ought to judge events in Bruges. Nevertheless, several specific developments also took place in the city, leaving a mark that is still visible today. The first of these was the maritime harbour project. Many nineteenth-century intellectuals and politicians argued that the city would be able to regain its past glory by building a new sea port. On 23 August 1895, the Belgian parliament finally approved the plans for such a harbour. The Maatschappij der Brugse Zeevaartinrichtingen (Bruges Association of Maritime Institutions – MBZ) was founded on 26 November that same year, and building commenced in 1896. The harbour was completed in 1904. In its original form, it consisted of an outer harbour, a curved dike (the famous môle) running for around 2.5 km and a sea-lock providing access to a canal linking the harbour of Zeebrugge directly with the docks at Bruges. The territory of the city had been extended significantly to the north and towards the coast in 1899 and 1901, when the municipality of Sint-Pieters-op-de-Dijk and large chunks of Dudzele, Koolkerke, Lissewege, Heist and Uitkerke were swallowed up by Bruges. By the turn of the century, therefore, the city once more bordered the sea. In the process, its 1840 surface area of 431 hectares rose to over 2,500 hectares.

The new port meant more to Bruges than just a major investment. The citizens of the town hoped that it would restore the prosperity they had last enjoyed in the Middle Ages. Constant reference was thus made to the city's mediaeval past during the immense celebrations that marked the opening of the harbour in the summer of 1907. The organisers put on a show that was to be repeated in later decades – a grandiose mediaeval tournament in the marketplace, a Golden Tree cortège and an exhibition devoted to the Golden Fleece. The people of Bruges continue to look on Zeebrugge as the key to their economic development and still hark back in their exhibitions, processions and publications to the city's mediaeval heyday. Following an encouraging start, it quickly became apparent that such immense expectations could not be realised, primarily because links with the hinterland still left a great deal to be desired. The Germans transformed Zeebrugge into a fully-fledged military port during the First World War, and then destroyed it prior to their retreat in 1918.

Zeebrugge was not the only major economic initiative to leave a lasting impression on city life. In the metallurgical sector, the nineteenth-century De Jaeghere iron-foundry was transformed into a new company, La Brugeoise, following a severe crisis in 1902. In 1905, the company settled between the Ghent-Bruges canal and the site of the railway station built in 1939. The workforce had grown to 1,500 by 1909, producing metal bridges and girders, trains, trams and other rolling stock. The firm still occupies the same site, but has since merged with the Bombardier company of Canada. Its workforce was sharply reduced in the 1980s and 1990s.

In 1897, decades before the trend towards foreign investment in Flanders began in earnest, the Nederlandsche Gist- and Spiritus-fabriek of Delft commenced operations in Bruges at the former Jules Verstraete distillery near Komvest. The Brugse Gistfabriek became Belgium's foremost producer of baker's yeast, and also manufactured alcohol. The company developed progressive social facilities for its employees, including decent housing. The plant was the only foreign company in the city centre – a location that inevitably gave rise to environmental problems from the 1970s onwards. The old factory, a remarkable structure in the Neue Sachlichkeit style, was demolished in 1985. The office buildings on Komvest date from 1925 and have an impressive Art Deco interior. The company's present factory is located at the docks, and has concentrated since the 1980s on the production of enzymes for use in detergents. Having undergone a series of mergers, it now belongs to Genencor International. Once again, the workforce has been sharply reduced in recent decades.

Despite these developments, Bruges could hardly have been called an industrial town, and the labour movement was slow to take off. Only a thousand families belonged to Socialist organisations in 1914, whereas Catholic bodies reached a much greater proportion of the

Art Deco interior of c. 1930 in the office building of the Brugse Gistfabriek

population, albeit due in many cases to social coercion. The Catholic population had to contend with dissent in its own ranks in the early part of the twentieth century, when the Kristene Volkspartij (Christian People's Party), led by the priest Edmond Fonteyne, enjoyed significant electoral success. After 1914, however, the party disappeared almost entirely from the political scene. Some of its supporters, including the future statesman Achilles Van Acker, joined the Socialists. The Catholic party continued to enjoy an absolute majority in the city for many years afterwards. Count Amedeé Visart de Bocarmé became burgomaster in 1876 and held the post until his death in 1924. He was succeeded by Victor Van Hoestenberghe, who remained in office until 1956, with an interruption in the period 1941-44.

The citizens of Bruges grew increasingly aware in the nineteenth century of their town's wealthy past – a process which continued after the turn of the century. The highlight was the Flemish Primitives

Jugendstil shopfront, c. 1900, Geldmuntstraat 9

exhibition in 1902, which provided a strong stimulus for academic research into local fifteenth-century painting. The exhibition was also extremely important in terms of the development of cultural tourism. Even today, large-scale exhibitions of this kind continue to stimulate tourism and research into local heritage. The 1902 exhibition promoted Bruges to its current status as one of Europe's most important cities of art.

To many people in the city, however, the glorious Middle Ages began to take on near-mythical proportions, which placed a heavy burden on the further development of local architecture. Bruges has few examples of Art Nouveau architecture, which was popular throughout Europe in around 1900. In the entire inner city, there are only three houses (Sint-Jacobsstraat 13 and O.-L.-Vrouwe-kerkhof-Zuid 6-8) and one shopfront (Geldmuntstraat 9) in this style. Neo styles were preferred until the 1970s, as they had been in the nineteenth century. Bruges in 1900 clearly lagged behind in its architectural development. When the new Stübben district to the north of the town centre was developed in 1897, preference was given to architecture in the Bruges style, based on the trends of the fourteenth to seventeenth century. The same happened in the 1930s when a residential district was built on horticultural land along Kruisvest and Rolweg. Architects even opted for a vieux-neuf style in the 1970s, during the construction of the Zilverpand, a residential and retail complex in the heart of the old town opposite Holy Saviour's Cathedral. Canon Adolf Duclos (1841-1925) played a significant part in this development. He published *L'art des façades à Bruges* in 1902, followed eight years later by his principal reference work, *Bruges, Histoire et souvenirs*. The two books had an overwhelming influence and were only superseded by other reference works in the field of conservation and local history in the last decade or so.

Clergymen like Duclos were important players in Bruges' cultural and social life. The city remained almost uniformly Catholic until well into the twentieth century. The bishopric was strictly ruled from 1895 to 1931 by Bishop Gustave Joseph Waffelaert, an extremely conservative prelate. Sunday Mass and popular worship remained highly vigorous in Bruges prior to 1914, as did Catholic education, newspapers and social groups. Members of the clergy remained very active in public life even after the influence of Church and religion had begun to wane dramatically, even in Bruges. Canon Achilles Logghe, the pioneer of the city's Christian labour movement, sat on the Public Assistance Committee from 1925 to 1959, becoming its chairman in 1953. The priest Antoon Viaene (1900-1979) was a historian of great merit, who organised several events, including the Golden Tree Processions. In his capacity as chairman of the Municipal Library's board of trustees, he had a profound influence on Bruges' cultural life. The current municipal library, De Biekorf, took its name from a journal, still published, which Viaene edited for some fifty years. Canon Jozef Dochy, who died in 1959, was the first chairman of the Friends of the Bruges Museums, which he helped found less than a year before his sudden death. This association, too, continues to play an important role in the city's cultural life.

Nevertheless, a few modest signs of secularisation were already apparent in the early twentieth century. Werkerswelzijn, a Socialist weekly newspaper for Bruges, first appeared in December 1901 and only ceased publication in 1992. The Brugsch Handelsblad, a neutral and independent weekly that is still published today, first appeared on 23 June 1906. The Vrije Burgersbond, an independent movement with primarily lower middle-class appeal, contested its first municipal elections in 1907. Its success was a source of concern for the Catholic party and the clergy.

The population of Bruges stood at almost 54,000 in 1914. The city had been officially Dutch-speaking since 1885, but public life continued to be dominated by French. Bruges was no longer the impoverished town it had been in 1850. The general standard of living had improved significantly, but some ten percent of the population remained illiterate. A little over ten percent was reliant on poor relief.

The German army invaded Belgium on 4 August 1914. Bruges was captured on 14 October, following a brief skirmish. The harsh

Onze-Lieve-Vrouwekerkhof-Zuid, numbers 6-8, Jugendstil double house-front, c. 1900

occupying regime lasted until 19 October 1918. The city was visited a week later by King Albert and Queen Elizabeth, who were welcomed by an excited and enthusiastic crowd. The harbour had been totally destroyed prior to the German retreat, several companies had been looted and virtually all the bridges around the city had been destroyed. The town centre survived the First World War unscathed, but the population had been obliged to endure four years of food shortages. A flu epidemic broke out in October 1918, killing 907 people in the town by December.

Bruges did not perform dynamically in either economic or demographic terms between the two World Wars. The city's population in 1930 was 2,500 fewer than in 1914, having declined to 51,400. No new companies of any note had been set up, although the Glasfabriek, which later became Glaverbel, was founded in Zeebrugge in 1925. Low wages attracted a few Antwerp diamond-polishing firms to Bruges and the surrounding districts. Harbour activity did not return to its pre-war level until 1927, and only unusual circumstances, such as the Antwerp dockers' strike in 1936, were able to bring about a temporary revival. There were some positive changes, however. New residential developments were built in the 1930s in the Sint-Anna area and the new district of Christus-Koning, which also gained a covered swimming pool. The world-famous Groeninge Museum, a new and surprisingly modern institution devoted to painting, was built in 1930, and an equally modern railway station was constructed on the edge of the city to replace the Neo-Gothic station on the Zand (1939). The architect Joseph Viérin, Alderman for Public Works between 1921 and 1938, was originally a defender of neo styles, but gradually came to support a more modern approach. The city council also sought to protect a large number of buildings and landscapes in the town centre by means of new legislation (1931). Central government was not prepared to accept the local proposals, however, because of their onerous financial implications. It was only in the 1970s and beyond that many of Bruges' buildings were given protected monument status. The city was, of course, modernised. An electricity supply was created in 1922, followed by mains water in 1923. Local society was also modernised. While the population of the town centre was declining, that of the outlying districts, especially Assebroek, Sint-Kruis and Sint-Andries, was growing strongly. The Dutch language steadily took hold in public life, but French retained its prestige as the language of the ruling class. The Catholic Action movement enabled the Church to strengthen its grip on believers, but attendance of Sunday Mass in Bruges had slipped to 54.5% by 1938. Only French-speaking Mouscroun and frivolous Ostend had lower attendance rates in West Flanders. Nevertheless, the Catholic majority on the city council remained invincible.

Tourism remained a crucial factor in the development of the city. The council had already embarked on the systematic promotion of tourism by 1919, and we have already referred to the opening of the new Groeninge Museum in 1930. The city authorities also organised a number of important exhibitions, including one of illuminated manuscripts and book-bindings in 1927 and, above all, a major

Memling exhibition in 1939. The focus in 1938 was on the general public. The Holy Blood Play, a grandiose religious spectacle centring on the famous local relic, drew thousands of visitors to Bruges. The mass, open-air event was staged four more times after the Second World War, with the final performance in 1962. It says much about the prevailing mentality of the city's administrators and opinion-makers that they sought for so long to stimulate tourism and to promote Bruges' image by staging mass religious spectacles.

Groeninge Museum, built in 1930 and surprisingly modern for Bruges

The German invasion in May 1940 was followed by another four years of occupation. Once again, it was the port of Zeebrugge that suffered most from the war, with the town centre remaining almost completely undamaged, although the Germans blew up several of the city gates prior to their retreat in September 1944. They also looted Michelangelo's famous Madonna and several paintings from Our Lady's Church. Fortunately, the items in question were recovered undamaged in 1945. Between 1942 and 1944, Bruges was merged with its outlying districts an experiment that was reversed as soon as the town was liberated. It nevertheless drew attention to the fact that an urban agglomeration now existed that was much larger than the historical city.

Bruges redoubled its efforts after the war to realise the ambitions it had cherished since the turn of the century. Zeebrugge harbour was rebuilt immediately after the Liberation in 1944. Even so, the level of traffic at Bruges-Zeebrugge in 1950 was less than half that in 1939. The subsequent process of expansion, however, virtually quadrupled activity by 1960 – a record year in which Zeebrugge finally surpassed its previous best performance in 1911. For the first time since the beginning of the twentieth century, the expansion of Zeebrugge was now carefully and systematically planned. The first stage ran from the 1960s to 1971 and was quick to bear fruit. Traffic measured in tons increased ten-fold between 1960 and 1975. Bruges, like other locations in Flanders, also managed to attract a wide variety of big companies and multinationals.

Tourism was another key focus of attention. The Holy Blood Play was staged on four further occasions, and 1958 saw the first five-yearly revival of the Golden Tree Procession, which evokes the Burgundian splendour of late-mediaeval Bruges. The Reie Festival, organised for the first time in 1959, was different in character. Hundreds of actors presented historical tableaux along the city canals and in the surrounding buildings. The ancient Holy Blood Procession was modernised, and a triennial exhibition for contemporary art shook up the staid citizens of Bruges in the 1960s. It was exhibitions of early art, however, like that of the

Anonymous Flemish Primitives (1969), which attracted the most attention internationally. The city's Tourist Service has mounted frequent information and promotional campaigns since the 1950s, using film, radio and television.

In spite of all these initiatives, Bruges has retained a small-town mentality in many respects. The 88-year-old burgomaster Victor Van Hoestenberghe remained in the saddle until 1956, when he finally responded to a gentle but clear hint dropped by the progressive bishop, Emiel Jozef Desmedt. His successor was Alderman Pierre Vandamme, who took office at the age of 61. Vandamme's principal concern was with the expansion of Zeebrugge harbour and the economic development that would spring from this. He was apparently unmoved by the decay and even destruction being suffered in the meantime by the town's cultural heritage, preferring to attract tourists by staging colourful events.

Nor was there any desire to mount new initiatives in outlying districts. Plans for a university were dropped in 1965, leaving the town with a lasting cultural handicap. The Europe College, founded in 1949, which trains young academics with an eye to European integration, adds a cosmopolitan flavour to Bruges outside the tourist season. The institution was one of the few cultural bright spots in small, post-war Bruges. Despite the economic boom of the 1960s, the towns population levelled off at around 50,000. The 1970s, however, saw the end of the old Bruges. Merger with the surrounding districts resulted in a new city of around 120,000 inhabitants. The following chapter is devoted to this most recent episode in Bruges' history.

Monument to Burgomaster Pierre Vandamme (1956-1971) at the Port of Zeebrugge

THE NEW CITY: BRUGES 1971-2000

Bruges merged with its surrounding municipalities in 1971, six years before a nation-wide wave of boundary-changes. Assebroek, Dudzele, Koolkerke, Lissewege, Sint-Andries, Sint-Kruis and Sint-Michiels all became part of Bruges, together with areas of Heist, Loppem, Oostkamp and Ramskapelle. In 1977, the parish of Vijve-Kapelle (formerly part of Sint-Kruis), with its important Neo-Gothic village centre, was transferred to the new municipality of Damme. The merger has made Bruges the third largest city in Flanders, with a population of almost 120,000. The city's first Socialist burgomaster, Frank Van Acker, was strongly in favour of the changes. He held the post from 1977 until his death in 1992, but the period covered by this chapter began with the Christian Democrats (CVP) winning a further six years in office at the 1970 local elections. The newly elected council was determined to make the most of the opportunities created by the municipal merger, and a wide variety of initiatives, plans and designs were drawn up. After only a few months in office, the 76-year-old burgomaster Pierre Vandamme was replaced by his party colleague Michel Van Maele, the former burgomaster of Sint-Michiels. Van Maele was a progressive civic leader, who presided over a great many important projects. His administration was tainted, however, by the suspicion of political racketeering and cronyism, leading to its defeat at the polls in 1976.

Nevertheless, several of his administration's achievements are still clearly visible in the cityscape a quarter of a century on. The cleaning up of the canals began in 1971. Today's visitors would be surprised to learn that only two and a half decades ago, the reien used to fill the town centre with a horrible stench every summer. Historical buildings continued to be lost until the 1960s and a pressing need arose to deal with derelict and empty properties in the town centre. The Marcus Gerards Foundation

De Caese. This house on Steenhouwersdijk formed part
of the Liberty of Bruges complex until 1988.
It was then sold to Paribas bank, which has thoroughly and tastefully restored it

was created in 1965 to publicise the problem, leading in 1971, immediately after the merger, to the setting up of the Municipal Conservation and Restoration Department. The new service was given the brief of developing a systematic approach to the protection and restoration of the historic town centre. Encouraged by Alderman Andries Vanden Abeele, who was responsible for urban renewal, a structural plan for the city was published in 1975. This plan, the first of its kind in Belgium, included a variety of progressive ideas, including the pedestrianisation of the inner city. Lack of time ultimately prevented Vanden Abeele from getting all the aspects of his plan enshrined in municipal policy.

A number of cultural stimuli were also felt in the 1970s. Since that time, summers in Bruges have drawn lovers of early music from all over the world. Work began on a new, contemporary building in Kuipersstaat to house the municipal library. A Museum of Folklore was set up in Balstraat, and the Guido Gezelle Museum in Rolweg was acquired and modernised by the city. The Golden Tree Procession, Reie Festivals and the annual Holy Blood Procession (revived in 1970) proved very successful. A one-off mediaeval tournament was held in the marketplace in 1974. Saint John's Hospital vacated its historical buildings in the city centre in 1976 and took up residence at new premises in Sint-Pieters. A major exhibition devoted to the institution's history focused attention on the potential of the now vacant complex. On the down side, there were no large-scale exhibitions of early art in Bruges in the 1970s and the final triennial for contemporary art was held in 1974. The involvement of the former peripheral municipalities in general city policy after 1971 had a significant impact. Local monuments outside the town centre began to attract more attention from visitors. The historic count's castle at Male, the location of Saint Trudo's Abbey since 1954, the Great Barn of Ter Doest Abbey and the historic village centre at Lissewege, the mediaeval Zeven Torentjes farm in Assebroek, Beisbroek Park in Sint-Andries and Boudewijnpark in Sint-Michiels all became tourist attractions. An important modern development occurred in the shape of a new football stadium in Sint-Andries. Initially called the Olympia and now the Jan Breydel Stadium, it hosts the home games of the city's two first-division teams, Club Brugge and Cercle Brugge.

None of this could save the CVP, however, which lost its absolute majority in the 1976 elections for reasons we have already noted. The coalition that took office in 1977 included all the city's political parties except the Christian Democrats, bringing to an end over a century of uninterrupted Catholic rule in Bruges. The new burgo-master, the Socialist Frank Van Acker, stamped his personal seal on the city council, enabling him to consolidate his position at successive municipal elections in 1982 and 1988. The Socialist Party (SP) became the city's strongest in 1988, but owed its success almost entirely to Van Acker's personality. When he died in 1992, he was succeeded for two years by his party colleague Fernand Bourdon. In the meantime, the CVP returned to power as the SP's coalition partner. It did not come as a great surprise, therefore, when the CVP once again became the biggest political grouping in the municipal council in 1994. The present burgo-master, Patrick Moenaert, who is in his forties, looks certain to head the administration until after the year 2000.

The development of Zeebrugge harbour has always remained above party politics. Virtually all the city's politicians, unions and businesses have been united in the importance they attach to the continuing expansion of the port of Bruges. The Belgian government decided in 1970 that Zeebrugge should be developed into a modern sea port, capable of meeting the transport needs that had evolved since the second half of the 1960s. A clear increase in scale was occurring, with the commissioning of large oil-tankers and bulk-carriers, and the spread of containerisation and roll-on/roll-off transport. So it was that an entirely new harbour was created at Zeebrugge between 1972 and 1984.

A new sea-lock was completed in 1983. It was 500 m long, 57 m wide and had a working depth of 18.5 m. The new back-harbour was constructed at more or less the same time, covering an area of 1,300 hectares and comprising a northern and a southern dock.

The quay areas are located around the docks, with cargo-handling terminals and storage and distribution facilities for goods, new cars and bulk products. The final part of the project was the impressive out-harbour, linked to the back-harbour by a sea-lock. The out-harbour is located in the sea, and is protected by two longitudinal dikes. It is directly accessible to large ocean-going vessels and is ideal for container and ro-ro transport. Its construction was one of the largest hydraulic engineering projects in the world. The new port of Zeebrugge was opened by King Baudouin in 1985.

This positive development was marred by a horrific disaster at Zeebrugge in 1987, when the British ferry Herald of Free Enterprise capsized. The accident cost 192 lives, most of them British. In the wake of the disaster, the UK government paid tribute to the rescue operations mounted from Bruges.

Greenery and contemporary art in the city centre:
Four Horsemen of the Apocalypse (Rik Poot) in the Hof Arents

Zeebrugge was still a small port in the 1960s, handling a maximum of 2 million tons of cargo a year. The figure in 1995, by contrast, was over 30 million tons. A great many companies have set up around the harbour, helping make it the biggest employer in the Bruges region, with some 25,000 jobs (direct and indirect). If the port is to continue developing in an optimum fashion, its communications with the hinterland will have to be further improved. This entails enhanced links with the European motorway, waterway and railway networks. A new station is planned for 1998, and improved rail links with the hinterland will be completed in 2005. Political consensus as to the manner in which the harbour's potential ought best to be unlocked has, however, evaporated.

In addition to the port, a second factor is crucial to Bruges future development, namely its cultural and historic heritage, which attracts several million visitors to the city every year. This consists in the first place of the exceptionally valuable and unusually well-preserved historic cityscape (as Marc Ryckaert put it in his *Historische Steden-atlas van België*, published in 1991). Then there is the impressive art collection in museums and libraries, churches and monasteries, public and private collections. Five major archives contain vital background information on these works, enabling researchers to place them in their proper European context. A further dimension was added in 1977 with the foundation of a Municipal Archaeo-logical Department, which raised the standard of research into the city's historically rich sub-soil. The department has achieved some sensational results over the past two decades. Excavations in the choir of Our Lady's Church in 1979 and 1980, prompted by the moving of the funeral monuments of Mary of Burgundy and Charles the Bold, revealed vital information about those masterpieces, but also uncovered a series of painted, mediaeval tombs. Ten years later, the department was instrumental in the discovery of the remains of the lost church of Saint Donatian's and the associated complex of buildings on the Burg.

The excavations on the Burg were prompted by the construction of a major hotel with an underground car park. The project highlighted the dilemmas facing an old city like Bruges. Modern architectural and planning ideas have to be reconciled with the need to preserve and develop the unique, historic city centre. Meanwhile, economic imperatives in terms of tourism and transport have to be met while ensuring that the town remains accessible and a pleasant place in which to live. Whereas public opinion had been almost unanimous in its support for the development of Zeebrugge, it was much more fragmented when it came to the issue of the historic town centre. The people of Bruges expressed their opinions and disagreements at crowded public meetings and through letters, submissions, campaign groups, pamphlets and brochures in the 1980s and 90s. If nothing else, it demonstrated the depth of the residents' concern for the development of their living and working environment. The city council has consistently taken account of the views of local people, with whom it maintains systematic contact by means of public meetings and enquiries. The policies pursued by the local authority in the fields of urban renewal, the development of tourism, traffic management, art and culture and the organisation of events have been the subject of intense debate and critical assessment by Bruges public opinion. Even so, Burgomaster Van Acker and his team achieved a great deal, often in the teeth of received wisdom. The first pedestrianised streets and squares, Sint-Amandstraat, Breidelstraat, Burgplein and Simon Stevinplein, date from Van Acker's first term (1977-82). The changes were part of a first transport plan, designed to tackle the steady increase in the volume of car traffic and the difficulty of parking. Several underground car-parks were constructed in the same period. Wide pavements and narrow roads were laid in the main shopping streets. And to the surprise of many, 1960s asphalt was systematically replaced with cobble-stones.

Urban renewal in the period 1977-94 was thus clearly focused on the public domain – streets, squares and parks. The effect was to give the old city centre a real face-lift. Pedestrians were able for the first time to stroll freely along the shopping streets and historic squares like the Burg and the Zand. On the other hand, surprisingly little attention was paid to cycle traffic in the 1980s and public transport experiments failed to yield the desired results, a situation that persisted until the early 1990s. Several new parks, purchased from private owners, added to the city's public greenery. Between 1977 and 1988, over 80,000 m² of streets were pedestrianised and provided with contemporary street furniture, benches, sculptures and lights, and a great deal of greenery. These moves came in for a great deal of criticism, including an expensively produced book published in 1985. Although ostensibly a new standard work, it launched a bitter polemic against the city council's supposed penchant for 'kitsch'. When the council finally got round to filling the empty niches on the facade of the Town Hall in 1983, the same author accused it of lacking any logic or elementary artistic sensibility and attempting to appease international artistic tourism. It has to be said that many of the recent sculptures installed in the city centre are not exactly challenging. Rather than acting as distinctive markers in the cityscape, they tend to be pleasant but safe street ornaments. Nevertheless, to call them 'organised kitsch' or 'nonsense', is going too far and does a great injustice to the people who commissioned them in an attempt to create a city centre that is attractive and a pleasant place to live.

The public domain also includes a number of buildings, such as the Town Hall and other administrative centres, schools, libraries, cultural centres, churches and museums. Once again, a systematic approach was adopted, adding value to such buildings in the final quarter of the twentieth century. The Town Hall on the Burg was given a thorough cleaning in the 1980s, culminating in the installation of the aforementioned statues in the previously empty niches. The Palace of the Liberty of Bruges was vacated in the 1980s by the law courts which had occupied the building since 1795. Having stood empty for a few years, the palace was taken over in 1988 by the municipal administration. Users of the tourist service are now received in a prestigious eighteenth-century room, formerly the Members' Chamber and office of the burgomaster of the Liberty of Bruges.

A brand-new, contemporary building was constructed for the city's law courts near Kruispoort, on the edge of the inner city, where an old barrack once stood. The site had been used for military purposes since the end of the eighteenth century, before which it was the location of the Carthusian monastery of Genadedal. The religious community was dissolved in 1783 by Emperor Joseph II, at which point the seventeenth and eighteenth-century buildings came into the possession of the state. Part of the old monastery complex survived, but was almost entirely disfigured until the construction of the new city law courts. The historic buildings on Langestraat were then restored, put to appropriate use and fully integrated in the very modern complex on Kruispoort. The overall development is a successful example of contemporary architecture incorporating restored historical buildings.

The city council chose to co-operate with the private sector on several occasions. It signed a leasing agreement with the Adornes Group for the operation of one of the city market-halls. This association of nine leading Bruges art-dealers has restored the market to its original

commercial function, selling works of art and housing several other important business and artistic activities. In 1985, the Kredietbank completed the restoration of the guildhouses belonging to Bruges cobblers and joiners in Steenstraat. The buildings were purchased in early 1976 by the city council for reasons of public utility, as part of a drive to renew the city centre. The new council handed the buildings over to the Kredietbank in June 1980, after the institution had

Modern law courts in Langestraat, incorporating historical monastery buildings

footed most of the bill for their restoration. Private institutions were also responsible in the 1980s and 90s for more important restoration projects. The most notable of these were the restoration of the mediaeval Genoese House in Vlamingstraat by the Generale Bank, the mediaeval Hof van Watervliet in Oude Burg by the Christelijk Ziekenfonds, the eighteenth-century house De Caese on Hoogstraat by the Paribas bank and the nineteenth-century Memling house in Sint-Jorisstraat by Roularta publishers. De Caese was originally part of the law courts on the Burg, and was sold by the city council after standing empty for several years. The Memling house came into the possession of Bruges Social Services in the 1980s, before its restoration. The nineteenth-century wards of old Saint John's Hospital were transformed into an art and conference centre by a private initiative. Former burgomaster Michel Van Maele was the driving force behind this initiative.

The Reie Festival, Golden Tree cortège and the one-off Mary of Burgundy Procession in 1981, continued to enliven the city centre.

Interest in the Holy Blood Procession on Ascension Day seems to have waned since the early 1980s, which is hardly surprising as the event has not changed since 1970 – the longest period without updating since the war. Contemporary events in the city centre have given rise to a great deal of public dispute. A large open-air theatre with a capacity of over a thousand seats was purchased in 1980 and erected in the Burg in the summer. It was primarily used for concerts of

Scene from the Holy Blood Procession.
Stabat Mater group girls mourning the death of Christ

easy-listening, popular music. The performances gave rise to such protests, however, that the theatre has not been used fully since the second half of the 1980s. Bruges people seem to have become a little more tolerant in the 1990s, as annual festivals of pop and world music in the Minnewater Park have become an established part of the cultural calendar. In the meantime, the city has retained its reputation as a centre of early music. The cultural repertoire was further extended a few years ago to include a third-world film festival. Solidarity with the developing world has also found fertile ground in Bruges in the shape of the many grassroots campaign groups in the city. Their work culminates in the annual Romero Memorial, organised for the first time in 1986. The 125 year-old city theatre has been incorporated in a new cultural centre, which is sure to become an important stimulus for artistic life in Bruges. The new structure has also created opportunities for initiatives in the field of contemporary art. Several major exhibitions of old art have been organised since the 1980s. The latest highpoint was the Memling exhibition in 1994, which attracted over 300,000 people.

Visitors to the inner city will be struck by the fact that there is very little architectural decay in Bruges, certainly since the 1980s. This is partly the result of the policy whereby home-improvement grants and vacancy taxes have helped enhance the inner-city environment. Vacant buildings in the town centre continue, however, to be a problem that constantly exercises the city council. In his first policy statement, Burgomaster Moenaert also raised the issue of vacant property above city shops.

Another noteworthy feature is the steady fall in Bruges population. The city had just under 116,000 inhabitants in 1995, representing a drop of around 3,500 since 1974. The declining city population is, of course, a phenomenon that is occurring across Flanders. Many people continue to aspire to a detached house with a big garden in the country. Bruges is also confronted by a number of other problems. The region as a whole has a working population of just over 121,000 people, 10.5% of whom were unemployed in 1992. That year also saw the end of falling unemployment since 1985. Many companies in the metallurgical sector, which provides over half the region's industrial employment, have had a difficult time in recent years. The same goes for the electronics sector. Many of these companies now also belong to multinational groups with decision-making centres based in other countries. A new dynamism is clearly needed to ensure the further development of the city and region. The port of Zeebrugge will continue to provide the driving force, as will the city's cultural and historical heritage. Both elements lend the city and region a European and international dimension. It will soon become apparent whether or not Bruges is capable of exploiting the opportunities that undoubtedly exist in these fields.

Zeebrugge, aerial photograph of the port installations (1990)

FOOTBALL IN BRUGES

Football has long played an important part in the social life of western Europe. Bruges is certainly no exception, boasting two first-division football teams, Club Brugge K.V. and Cercle Brugge K.S.V. Both teams have existed for over a hundred years and have deep historical roots. The rise of football in Bruges owed much to the strong British influence in the town in the late nineteenth century.

Club Brugge was founded in 1890. Its early history was rather confused, but a series of splits and mergers ended in 1897 when Football Club Brugeois merged with Brugsche Football Club. The board of directors came under the influence at the turn of the century of the Liberal party and the Masonic Lodge, La Flandre. In the 1930s, it was the turn of the Socialists to dominate the board of the blue-and-blacks. The ideological element diminished sharply after the Second World War, although the club retained its working-class support, centred on a number of local pubs. Supporters' organisations flourished in the 1960s and 70s. Club Brugge, too, has had to face the problem of crowd violence since the 1980s, but the city's police have responded very effectively. Club has had a mixed history on the field as well. It did not win its first league title until the 1919-20 season, having had to make do with second place in 1911, when the championship was snatched by arch-rivals Cercle, following a local derby. Club then had to wait until 1972-73 to win its second title. Since then, however, Club Brugge has been one of Belgium's top teams, winning the league in 1975-76, 1976-77, 1977-78, 1979-80, 1989-90, 1991-92 and 1995-96. It has also played in a variety of European cup competitions since 1967.

Green and black Cercle Brugge was founded in 1899 by old boys of the Xaverian school in Mariastraat. The board was strongly influenced by the conservative wing of the Catholic Party. Although football is naturally a working-class sport, Cercle supporters have traditionally been more sober and middle-class in character. Like Club, Cercle Brugge has enjoyed varying success and has been significantly weaker than its rival since the 1960s. It is currently one of a group of first-division teams that never seems to quite make it to the very top. Cercle was Belgian champion in 1910-11, 1926-27 and 1929-30. Its low-point came in the 1965-66 season when it was demoted to the third division following a match-rigging scandal. Since then, Cercle has won the Belgian Cup in 1985.

The two teams took up residence at a brand-new stadium in the former district of Sint-Andries in 1975, following a campaign waged by the then burgomaster, Michel Van Maele. Van Maele had sat on Club's board since 1973, and continued to be one of its driving forces for many years. Another board member, Michel D'Hooghe, was appointed chairman of the Belgian Football League in 1987. The city will soon begin preparations for Euro 2000, as Bruges stadium will be the only one in Flanders to stage European Championship games in the year 2000. The event will permanently fix Bruges reputation as a football town.

TRAFFIC IN BRUGES

Traffic management and care for the environment have been
at the heart of city policy since the 1970s. The transport issue is
a complex one. The council has to ensure mobility and safety
while protecting the environment of the historic town centre.
Bruges has a maze of narrow streets with a great many valuable
buildings. Consequently, the steady growth of car traffic could not
be tolerated if the city's residents and heritage were to receive the
protection they deserved.

The first steps towards a managed traffic policy for the entire city
centre were taken in the 1972 structural plan. Its proposals and
blueprints were revolutionary for the time: cars had to behave like
pedestrians, public transport with smaller buses was to be given
priority, cycles were described as the ideal mode of urban transport,
the city centre had to be pedestrianised and a centrifugal parking
policy was promised that would progressively remove visiting cars
from the town centre. Concrete steps were not taken until the late
1970s, when the first pedestrianised streets were created as part of
the 1978 traffic plan. Paid parking and underground car parks are
now common features, but they were novelties at first and aroused
a good deal of resistance. Nevertheless, the results of the first traffic
plan were impressive, with a spectacular fall in the number of road
accidents. The first traffic plan took little account, however, of cycle
traffic. Nor was the city-bus experiment a great success.

The second traffic plan for the city centre dated from 1992 and was combined with traffic-taming plans for the outer districts. Key elements of the project were a new 30 km/hour speed limit in the city centre, a strict loop system, which made it virtually impossible to cross the city by car, the discouragement of tourist coaches and long-stay parking in the city centre, the stimulation of cycle and pedestrian traffic and the optimisation of public transport. This required close co-operation with the bus company De Lijn. An even more rigorous traffic plan for the city centre will be introduced during a second stage beginning in 1997. A parking-free Markt will lose its role as central traffic interchange, plugging the final gaps in the loop system. Henceforward, the city centre will be almost traffic-free, safe and accessible. The experience of the past years has shown that the number of road accidents will fall, use of public transport and cycles will increase and the accessibility of the centre will be guaranteed, with considerably fewer traffic jams. This means, of course, that parking – especially for longer periods – will have to occur on the edge of town. A large car park near the station opened in 1994, and the national railway company, NMBS, is now also closely involved in the development of the city's transport policy. As the second half of the 1990s proceeds, a great deal of money is being invested in the new station forecourt. City council, NMBS and De Lijn are all working together to control the flow of traffic into and out of Bruges by means of large car parks, well-organised public transport and proper attention to cyclists and pedestrians.

GREENERY IN BRUGES

Bruges City Council manages no fewer than 550 hectares of woods, parks and public squares. This green heritage adds a very special touch to the cityscape. Bruges has long boasted a number of large, open spaces within the area defined by the 1297 city walls. Only the very earliest nucleus of the town is lacking in greenery. Bruges once had a great many kitchen gardens, which together accounted for around half the towns surface area. The majority of this land was, however, built on in the twentieth century. There were also forty large monastery gardens at the end of the eighteenth century. Several municipal parks, Sebrechts Park, Sincfal Park and, above all, the large Astrid Park owe their existence to a former monastery garden. Other parks were laid on the site of the bleaching-fields once used by the linen industry. Koning Albert Park, Minnewater Park and Hof de Jonghe (Lange Rei) were originally bleaching-fields. Archery clubs like the Guilds of Saint Sebastian and Saint George still have extensive land in Bruges, although these green oases alongside Kruisvest are not open to the public. The town centre is literally surrounded by a green belt, formed by the line of the old fortifications which meander almost uninterrupted around the town. The Municipal Parks Service also takes care of trees, shrubbery and flowers in the city streets and squares. Attractive examples are the greenery on the Burg, the banks of several canals, the Begijnhof, Vlamingstraat and the Zand.

Visitors and residents can find plenty of public parks and woods outside the old town, too. Most were created around historic buildings. The 140-hectare Beisbroek and Tudor estates in Sint-Andries are particularly important, while a popular children's farm has grown up at Zeven Torentjes centred around a mediaeval pigeon-loft in Assebroek. Nor should we overlook the provincial estate at Tillegem in Sint-Michiels, where the château, originally a mediaeval water-fortress, now serves as the base of Westtoerisme, the provincial tourist authority. The woods, extending over almost

55 hectares, have been open to the public since the 1960s. The Bruges region as a whole still boasts a great deal of woodland and green areas, certainly compared to the rest of the province.

Special mention ought to be made here of the two municipal cemeteries. The old central burial ground at Steenbrugge-Assebroek is more than two hundred years old and owes its existence to an edict of Emperor Joseph II. In the nineteenth century, Bruges Cemetery was turned into a romantic park, with stately avenues of beeches, Neo-Gothic monuments and plentiful greenery. The construction of a lapidary, the restoration of important tombs and the publication of a professional guide has made the cemetery attractive to ordinary visitors. The new park cemetery, the Blauwe Toren, was laid in 1976. The conception of this burial place, with its crematorium, columbarium and field for the scattering of ashes reflects changes in Western ideas about death and funerals. The park is dominated by a monumental contemporary sculpture by Hubert Minnebo.

Zeven Torentjes children's farm in Assebroek,
a new role for a historic farm with its mediaeval pigeon loft

1. *Zeebrugge* Front and back-harbour with sea-lock and Boudewijn Canal to Bruges.
2. *Ter Doest*, (Lissewege) 13th-century barn of the former Cistercian Abbey.
3. *Damme* Mediaeval foreport of Bruges.
4. *Vijve Kapelle* Neo-Gothic village centre.
5. *Male* Count's castle, 12th century, now Saint Trudo's Abbey.
6. *Ryckevelde* European study centre in an attractive natural setting.
7. *Zeven Torentjes* Farm with mediaeval pigeon-loft, now a children's farm.
8. *Jan Breydel-stadion* Home ground of Club and Cercle Brugge.
9. *Boudewijnpark* Leisure park.
10. *Tillegem* 14th-century water-fortress in wooded surroundings.
11. *Beisbroek and Tudor* Municipal parks (with observatory) in former heathland.

1 *Town Hall*
Late 13th-century (originally the count's prison or Ghiselhuus), now the seat of the modern city council. The current late-Gothic building with its stone facade dates chiefly from the period 1376-86.

2 *Recorder's House*
Once part of the municipal administration. Unique combination of Gothic and Renaissance elements in the facade, 1537.

3 *Palace of the Liberty of Bruges*
Home from the late Middle Ages of the council of the Liberty of Bruges, the rural territory around the town. The current Classical building was built in 1722 and is now used as the city's Administrative Centre.

4 *Proosdij*
Administrative and judicial seat of the double lordship of Saint Donatian's, built in the Baroque style, 1665-66.

5 *Belfry and Halle*
Belfry (tower 83 m high) and market-hall, late 13th – early 14th century. Symbol of the strength and autonomy of the mediaeval city.

6 *Provincial Hall*
Seat of the province of West Flanders, Neo-Gothic (1892), on the site of the former Waterhalle.

7 *Fishmarket*
Classical market buildings, built in the Dutch period (1820-21).

8 *Law Courts*
Major new project (designed 1979) incorporating historical Carthusian monastery buildings.

9 *Tolhuis*
Used to administer taxes on merchandise during the *Ancien Régime*. Built in 1477-78 by the then holder of the tax privilege at Sint-Jansbrug.

10 *Poortersloge*
Gothic building with decorative tower, 15th century. Meeting place for privileged merchants. Now part of the National Archive.

11 *Berg van Charitate*
Municipal bank (literally Mountain of Charity) which offered interest-free loans (founded 1573, located here from 1629 to the end of the 18th century). Also used for poor relief in the 19th century, now the Provincial Land Registry.

12 *Augustijnenbrug*
Mediaeval stone bridge over the Augustijnen-rei. Built in the 14th century near the original city walls on the initiative of the nearby Augustinian monastery. Merchandise was once displayed on the old stone benches.

13 *State Teacher Training College*
Large Neo-Gothic building (L. Delacenserie, 1884) on the site of the former shooting range of the Guild of Saint George.

14 *Prinsenhof*
Count's residence in the town (1396), substantially remodelled in the late-Burgundian period. The present complex is largely of a later date.

15 *Nieuw Waterhuis* 18th-century building between the inner and outer defensive canals, built as part of a water distribution system dating back to the Middle Ages. Drew water from several sources including the canals.

Guild-houses
16 *Bakers'*
Steenstraat 19

17 *Masons*
Steenstraat 25

18 *Tanners*
Huidevettersplein 10

19 *Cobblers*
Steenstraat 40

20 *Joiners*
Steenstraat 38

Windmills
There were dozens of windmills on the city walls until the 19th century. They are re-called by the following mills on Kruisvest:

21 *Sint-Janshuismolen*
Only authentic Bruges mill

22 *Bonne Chieremolen*

23 *Nieuwe Papegaai*

24 *De Nieuwe Coelewey*

City gates and fortifications
25 *Defensive tower in the original city ramparts*
Remnant of the first city walls (1127) on Augustijnenrei.

Monumental gates into the city were incorporated in the second or great ramparts (1297).
Four gates and one defensive tower have survived:

26 *Ezelpoort*

27 *Kruispoort*

28 *Gentpoort*

29 *Smedenpoort*

30 *Poertoren*

Industrial architecture
31 *Mouterij Cauwe* Oostmeers, Maltings on Kapucienenreitje, 1888, recently converted into houses.

32 *Warehouses* Komvest, Built in the second half of the 18th century at the town dock. Initiative of the Bruges Chamber of Commerce. Large sections have been demolished.

33 *Yeast factory* Office building with Art Deco interior, 1925. The original factory building was demolished in 1985.

Parish churches

① *Saint Anne's Church* Late-Gothic hall church (1621!) with Baroque furnishings.

② *Saint Mary Magdalene's Church* Neo-Gothic church (1851-53) on the site of the former Franciscan monastery. Successor of Saint Catherine's, outside the city walls, which was demolished in 1578.

③ *Our Lady's Church* Independent parish since 1116. First church built in the 9th century. Three-aisled cross church from the 13th century, largely Scheldt Gothic.

④ *Saint Giles' Church* Parish church since the mid-13th century. Converted into a three-aisled hall church in the second half of the 15th century.

⑤ *Saint James' Church* Parish church since the mid-13th century. Three-aisled, late-Gothic church with heavy crossing tower.

⑥ *Holy Saviour's Church* The first church in Bruges (9th century). Three-aisled cross church, French influenced and with several surviving Romanesque features. Cathedral (bishop's seat) since 1834.

⑦ *Saint Walburga's Church* Pure Baroque church (1619-43) of the former Jesuit monastery, inspired by the Gesù Church in Rome.

Other churches and chapels

⑧ *Sacred Heart Church* Neo-Gothic, former Jesuit church (1879-85). Now used as a theatre.

⑨ *Jerusalem Chapel* Chapel devoted to the Holy Sepulchre (147183) and intended as a replica of the Church of the Holy Sepulchre in Jerusalem. Founded (1427) by the Bruges-Genoese Adornes family.

⑩ *Joseph Ryelandt Hall* Former convent church of the Discalced Carmelite nuns, taken over by Anglicans in 1820 to serve Bruges' large English colony. Restored in 1983 and turned into a municipal concert hall (Joseph Ryelandt Hall).

⑪ *Candlemakers Chapel* Originally Saint Peter's Chapel, supposedly founded by Robert the Frisian. Demolished in the 18th century and partially taken over by the Candlemakers Chapel. Now used for Protestant and Anglican services.

⑫ *Saint Basil's Chapel* Chapel of the count's castle built in the 12th century in the indigenous Romanesque style. The upper church, the Chapel of the Holy Blood, which still houses the mediaeval relic, has been remodelled many times over the centuries.

⑬ *Actors' Chapel* Built in 1421. Restored some considerable time ago and used by free-thinking societies.

Monasteries and convents

⑭ *Poor Clares* Founded in 1469 through the mediation of Lodewijk van Gruuthuse. The nuns left in 1990.

⑮ *Beghards* Male counterparts of beguines, active in the textile industry from the 13th century. The movement died out in the early 16th century, and the city magistrates founded a school for poor children in the monastery buildings (1513). Became the Municipal Academy of Art in 1891.

⑯ *Dominican nuns* Founded outside the city (Engelendale) in the 13th century. Moved inside the walls (Jacobinessenstraat) at the end of the sixteenth century, and then to Vlamingdam in 1861.

⑰ *Abbey of the Dunes* Cistercian Abbey of the Dunes, founded in Koksijde in the 12th century. Moved into the city in the 17th century where it occupied a new abbey (17th century with 18th-century church). Episcopal Seminary since 1833.

⑱ *English Convent* Founded in 1629 by English nuns (canonesses regular) and built in the 17th-18th century (monumental domed church, 1736-39).

⑲ *Saint Godelieve Abbey* Benedictine convent, founded in Gistel in 12th century; moved into the city in the late 16th century. Located in Boeveriestraat since 1623.

⑳ *Capuchins* Founded in 1592. Originally located on the southern side of the Zand until the laying of the railway and building of the station (1838, 1865). Housed in the current 19th-century monastery buildings since 1869.

㉑ *Carthusians* Founded in 1318 outside the city walls. Moved into the city in 1609, taking occupation of the converted Saint Aubert's Hospice. Abolished in 1783. The buildings were then used as a barracks before being incorporated in the new law courts.

㉒ *Carthusian nuns* Founded in around 1348 outside the town. Moved into the city at the end of the 16th century, where the refuge was converted into a convent (17th century). It is now occupied by Social Services and the church is used as a military chapel.

㉓ *Maricolen* Founded as a community of spiritual daughters in Rozendal in the 17th century. Developed into a fully-fledged monastic community which moved into its current premises in 1804. Involved in education.

㉔ *Discalced Carmelites* Founded in 1630-31. At current location since 1633 (former Hof van Uitkerke).

㉕ *Discalced Carmelite nuns* Also known as Theresians, founded in 1626. Ended up at current location in 1833 after occupying a variety of premises (including Joseph Ryelandt concert hall).

㉖ *Sarepta* Augustinian canonesses, founded in Biervliet in the 15th century. After a series of moves, the community settled in Bruges in 1617 (converted Hof van Sint-Pol). Abolished in 1784. Since used for educational purposes in partially renewed buildings.

㉗ *Spermalie* Cistercian Convent, founded c.1200 in Sint-Pieterskapelle. Moved into the city in the late 16th century, but only occupied current location in 1607, following the conversion of the Duinen-hof (refuge of the Abbey of the Dunes). Abolished in 1796 and now integrated in the large educational establishment of the same name.

㉘ *Black Sisters* Active in healthcare (plague-victims) from the 14th century, initially at Nieuwe Gentweg, then from 1807 at the Woensdagmarkt, where the Saint Francis-Xavier Hospital was extended.

Foreign merchants headquarters

1 *House of the Florentine Merchants* Academiestraat 1, Used from 1420 by the Florentines. The late-mediaeval building (shortly after 1430) is barely recognisable from the outside.

2 *Genuese Loge* Vlamingstraat 33, Built in 1399. Used as a serge hall from the departure of the Genoese from Bruges (c. 1522) until the 18th century. The current bell-tower dates from the later period (1720). Now a cultural centre.

3 *Oosterlingenhuis* Krom Genthof 1, Occupied by merchants of the German Hansa (Easterlings), whose presence in the city dated back to the 13th century. Built in 1478-81 and partially demolished in 18th century.

Dwelling houses

4 *Bouchoute* Markt 15, Impressive late-mediaeval house with high brick facade (c. 1480) crowned with a 17th-century weather-vane.

5 *De Crone* Sint-Jansstraat 7B, Monumental townhouse (once a wine-tavern) built in the Gothic style in around 1500.

6 *Gruuthuse* Dijver 17, Mansion built and converted in the 15th century by Lodewijk van Gruuthuse. Thoroughly restored in around 1900.

7 *Hof Bladelin* Naaldenstraat 19, Large townhouse with stair tower built by Pieter Bladelin, confidant of the dukes of Burgundy (mid-15th century). Used after 1469 by the Medici family of Italian bankers.

8 *Hof van Gistel* Naaldenstraat 7, Large townhouse built by Antoine de Bourbon, duke of Vendôme and lord of Gistel. The family long held an important tax-collecting privilege.

9 *Hof van Watervliet* Oude Burg 27, Originally the Hof van Sint-Joris (built by Chevalier Jan III de Baenst, lord of Sint-Joris-ten-Distel, mid-15th century). Converted in the 16th century by Marc Laurin, lord of Watervliet and renowned Humanist.

10 *De Halleux House* Oude Burg 21, 19th-century Neo-Classical townhouse with 18th-century orangery opening onto the Dijver.

11 *De la Torre House* Spanjaardstraat 16, Richly decorated facade with stone entrance gate in pure Renaissance style (mid-16th century).

12 *De Malvenda House* Wollestraat 53, Rich townhouse in late-Gothic style (late 15th, early 16th century) with window bays in continuous niches. Occupied in the 16th century by the Spanish magistrate Juan Perez de Malvenda.

13 *De Patientie* Spinolarei 2, 14th-century townhouse with original murals discovered in 1994.

14 *Ter Beurse* Vlamingstraat 35, Inn and bureau de change operated by the Van der Beurse family, with reconstructed brick facade from 1453 (date in old stone tablet).

15 *Zwart Huis* Kuipersstraat 23, Monumental house with brick facade, 15th century.

16 *Boomgaardstraat 7*, Late-Gothic stepped gable of c. 1500, in which each window bay is set in a separate, continuous niche.

17 *Geldmuntstraat 9*, Decorative Jugendstil shop-front.

18 *Genthof 7*, Double, cantilevered wooden facade with brick lower section. One of the two surviving wooden fronts in the town, 15th-16th century (see no. 29)

19 *Grauwwerkersstraat 2-4*, Original 13th-century facade. Primarily recent reconstruction from the 1980s.

20 *Koningin Elisabethlaan 2-98*, Large houses (boulevard architecture), chiefly late-19th and early 20th century, including contemporary styles.

21 *Nieuwstraat 8*, House with Gothic facade of 1530, the bays of which are set in a broken, composite arch (so-called Third Bruges facade type).

22 *Onze-Lieve-Vrouw Kerkhof Zuid 6-8*, Jugendstil facade of 1904.

23 *Oude Burg 33*, Sober Renaissance facade of 1571.

24 *Oude Zomerstraat 2*, House with narrow, prestigious facade (c. 1500) which is higher than the roof behind.

25 *Scheepsdalelaan 2*, Rare example of Art Deco style, 1932.

26 *Sint-Annarei 11*, Restored dwelling incorporating contemporary elements.

27 *Sint-Annarei 22*, Large merchant's house in Rococo style from the third quarter of the 18th century.

28 *Sint-Jacobsstraat 13*, Jugendstil facade.

29 *Vlamingstraat 90 (Korte Winkel)*, 16th-century wooden facade. One of only two surviving wooden fronts in Bruges (see no. 18).

30 *Vlamingstraat 100*, Unusual cantilevered brick bay window, built for the goldsmith Herman van Houtvelde in the early 16th century.

❶ *Prinselijk Begijnhof*
Largest beguinage, with a typically mediaeval,
enclosed structure. Used since 1927 by
Benedictine nuns.

❷ *Saint John's Hospital*
Founded in the mid-12th century. The three
surviving mediaeval wards (13th – early 14th
century) remained in use until the mid-19th
century.

❸ *Potterie Hospital* Mediaeval foundation
(first recorded in 1276) which developed into
a modern old peoples' home.

Almshouses
Houses founded privately to support elderly,
needy citizens. The most important ones are:

❹ *Rooms Convent*

❺ *Goderickx Convent*

❻ *Sint-Joos Almshouse*

❼ *Onze-Lieve-Vrouw van Blindekens*

❽ *Van Pamel Almshouse*

❾ *Marius Voet Almshouse*

❿ *Laurentia Soutieu Almshouse*

⓫ *De Moor Almshouse*

⓬ *Van Volden Almshouse*

⓭ *De Muelenaere Almshouse*

⓮ *Sint-Jozef Almshouse*

⓯ *Onze-Lieve-Vrouw van de Zeven Weeën*
Almshouse

⓰ *De Fontaine Almshouse*

⓱ *De Pelikaan Almshouse*

⓲ *De Vos Almshouse*

⓳ *Almshouse of the Tailors Guild*

⓴ *Almshouse of the Bakers Guild*

1 *Bruges National Archive*
Academiestraat 14-18

2 *Bruges Municipal Archive*
Burg 11a

3 *De Biekorf Municipal Public Library*
Kuipersstraat 3

Municipal Museums

4 *Arentshuis (Brangwyn Museum)*
Dijver 16

5 *Groeninge Museum*
Dijver 12

6 *Gruuthuse Museum*
Dijver 17

7 *Guido Gezelle Museum*
Rolweg 64

8 *Memling Museum (Saint John's Hospital)*
Mariastraat 38

9 *Potterie Museum*
Potterierei 79

10 *Museum of Folklore*
Rolweg 40

11 *Cultural Centre*
Sint-Jacobsstraat 20-26

12 *De Biekorf: civic hall*
Kuipersstraat 3

13 *Municipal Theatre*
Vlamingstraat 38

14 *De Korre Theatre*
Boterhuis – Sint-Jacobsstraat 62

15 *Old Saint John's Art and Conference Centre*
Mariastraat 38

16 *Europe College*
Dijver 11

17 *Provincial Information Centre, Archive and Library*
Jan van Eyckplein 1 (planned)

There is certainly no shortage of reference works or detailed studies devoted to Bruges. Modern Bruges historiography begins with A. DUCLOS, *Bruges. Histoire et souvenirs*, Bruges, 1910, and reprinted in 1976. It has now been entirely superseded, however, by J.A. VAN HOUTTE, *De geschiedenis van Brugge*, Tielt-Bussum, 1982 and M. RYCKAERT, *Historische stedenatlas van België: Bruges*, Brussels, 1991.

Three impressive works have been written or edited by V. VERMEERSCH, *Bruges. A Thousand Years of Art*, Antwerp, 1981, Idem (ed.), *Bruges and the Sea. From Bryggia to Zeebrugge*, Antwerp, 1983; Idem (ed.), *Bruges and Europe*, Antwerp, 1992.

A major book on Bruges seems to appear almost every year, shedding new light on one or more aspects of local history. A great many articles are also published, often in international journals and anthologies. Two recent examples can be found in *Peasants and Townsmen in Medieval Europe. Studia in honorem Adriaan Verhulst*, Ghent, 1995: *Les origines et l'histoire de Bruges: l'état de la question et quelques données nouvelles* (p. 117-133), by M. RYCKAERT, and *Stages of Economic Decline: late-medieval Bruges* (p. 259-270) by R. VAN UYTVEN. A bibliography of Bruges history has been compiled by A. VANHOUTRYVE, *Bibliografie van de geschiedenis van Brugge*, Bruges, 5 volumes, beginning in 1970.

The following are also worthy of mention, as they focus on a number of less well-known aspects of Bruges history: E. VANDEVYVERE, *Watervoorziening te Brugge van de 13de tot de 20ste eeuw*, Bruges, 1983; F. BONNEURE, *Brugge beschreven. Hoe een stad in teksten verschijnt*, Brussels, 1987; *Beeldig Brugge. Foto's en prentbriefkaarten, 1875-1900*, Bruges, 1987 (modest exhibition catalogue produced by the Municipal Archive, which provides a good insight into the social history of Bruges in the nineteenth century via a few deft sketches.); L. CONSTANDT et al., *Stenen herleven. 111 jaar 'kunstige herstellingen' in Brugge, 1877-1988*, Bruges, 1988, places urban conservation in Bruges in its precise political and social context; N. GEIRNAERT (ed.), *Brugge door de lens. Foto's en fotografen, 1900-1918*, Bruges, 1993, includes an important study by J. D'HONDT, *Brugge op de drempel van de twintigste eeuw* (p. 9-19).